To the Reader:

Scientology® applied religious philosophy contains pastoral counseling procedures intended to assist an individual to gain greater knowledge of self. The mission of the Church of Scientology is a simple one: to help the individual achieve greater self-confidence and personal integrity, thereby enabling him to really trust and respect himself and his fellow man. The attainment of the benefits and goals of Scientology philosophy requires each individual's dedicated participation, as only through his own efforts can he achieve these.

This book is part of the religious literature and works of the Scientology Founder, L. Ron Hubbard. It is presented to the reader as a part of the record of his personal research into life, and the application of same by others, and should be construed only as a written report of such research and not as a statement of claims made by the Church or the Founder.

Scientology philosophy and its forerunner, Dianetics® spiritual healing technology, as practiced by the Church, address only the "thetan" (spirit). Although the Church, as are all churches, is free to engage in spiritual healing, it does not, as its primary goal is increased spiritual awareness for all. For this reason, the Church does not wish to accept individuals who desire treatment of physical or mental illness but prefers to refer these to qualified specialists of other organizations who deal in these matters.

The Hubbard® Electrometer is a religious artifact used in the Church confessional. It in itself does nothing, and is used by ministers only, to assist parishioners in locating areas of spiritual distress or travail.

We hope the reading of this book is only the first stage of a personal voyage of discovery into this new and vital world religion.

Church of Scientology International

This Book Belongs to:

_____

_____
(Date)

L. RON HUBBARD

Handbook For
PRECLEARS

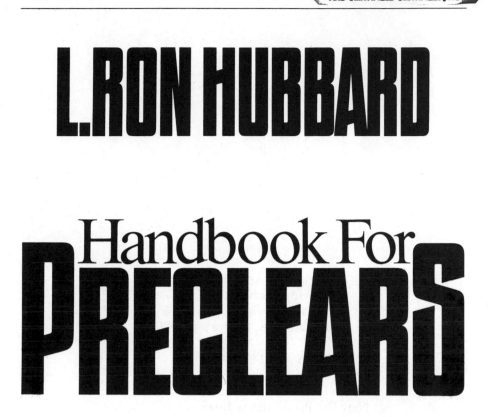

Bridge

PUBLICATIONS, INC.

Published in the U.S.A. by
Bridge Publications, Inc.
4751 Fountain Avenue
Los Angeles, California 90029

ISBN 0-88404-420-3

Published in other countries by
New Era Publications International, ApS
Store Kongensgade 55
1264 Copenhagen K, Denmark

ISBN 87-7336-606-4

Printed in the United States of America

Important Note

In reading this book, be very certain you never go past a word you do not fully understand.

The only reason a person gives up a study or becomes confused or unable to learn is because he or she has gone past a word that was not understood.

The confusion or inability to grasp or learn comes AFTER a word that the person did not have defined and understood.

Have you ever had the experience of coming to the end of a page and realizing you didn't know what you had read? Well, somewhere earlier on that page you went past a word that you had no definition for or an incorrect definition for.

Here's an example. "It was found that when the crepuscule arrived the children were quieter and when it was not present, they were much livelier." You see what happens. You think you don't understand the whole idea, but the inability to understand came entirely from the one word you could not define, *crepuscule*, which means twilight or darkness.

It may not only be the new and unusual words that you will have to look up. Some commonly used words can often be misdefined and so cause confusion.

This datum about not going past an undefined word is the most important fact in the whole subject of study. Every subject you have taken up and abandoned had its words which you failed to get defined.

Therefore, in studying this book be very, very certain you never go past a word you do not fully understand. If the material becomes confusing or you can't seem to grasp it, there will be a word just earlier that you have not understood. Don't go any further, but go back to BEFORE you got into trouble, find the misunderstood word and get it defined.

Definitions

As an aid to the reader, words most likely to be misunderstood have been defined in footnotes the first time they occur in the text. Words sometimes have several meanings. The footnote definitions in this book only give the meaning that the word has as it is used in the text. Other definitions for the word can be found in a dictionary.

A glossary including all the footnote definitions is at the back of this book. This glossary is not meant as a substitute for a dictionary.

The *Dianetics and Scientology Technical Dictionary* and *Modern Management Technology Defined* are both invaluable tools for the student. They are available from your nearest Scientology church or mission, or directly from the publisher.

Contents

How to Use This Book

This volume of self processing is designed for use in any of four ways:

1. As a workbook to be used wholly by the auditor[1] on the preclear,[2] or

2. As a homework book to be given the preclear for use between sessions, or

3. As a process done by the preclear himself with only occasional auditor help, or

4. As a processing manual used wholly by the preclear without an auditor.

The last use is possible, particularly when the preclear knows considerable about this science from other sources. But it

---

1. **auditor:** a person trained and qualified in applying Dianetics processes and procedures to individuals for their betterment; called an auditor because *auditor* means *one who listens.*

2. **preclear:** a spiritual being who is now on the road to becoming Clear, hence pre-Clear.

is possible, by reading this book alone, with considerable stamina, to carry straight on through.

If this book is given to you by an auditor, he expects to be consulted concerning any difficult points and he expects to run out your service facsimile when the time comes by Effort Processing.

The intention of this book is to increase your reaction time, improve your health and efficiency, to extend your life and to immunize you against illnesses. This book is not intended for the people who would usually seek help by reason of severe aberration,[3] neurosis or insanity: These should be worked upon by an auditor.

The optimum individual to which this book would be addressed for total self use would be a person capable of considerable action, such as a member of the armed services, a jet pilot, an artist, a musician desiring to speed his playing time and increase his ability. The address of this volume is to the person who, though normal enough would like to excel physically and mentally. An engineer, for instance, using this volume, could increase his ability to calculate and perform many times over.

Don't confuse this science with psychotherapy, psychosis or neurosis. Just because it handles these easily for the first time in history is no reason it is devoted to the lame, the halt and the aberrated. This science has as one of its branches the improvement of human ability above what it has been. This book was written to improve the ability of the able.

---

3. **aberration:** a departure from rational thought or behavior. From the Latin, *aberrare*, to wander from; Latin, *ab*, away, *errare*, to wander. It means basically to err, to make mistakes, or more specifically to have fixed ideas which are not true. Aberration is opposed to sanity, which would be its opposite.

Anyone using this volume as written can increase his skills, rehabilitate his goals and improve himself considerably above his fellows. We need people like that if we are going to have a better world.

Use this book as written. Don't try to combine it with old time mumbo-jumbo. Gasoline and alcohol, this book and psychiatry mix similarly. Use this book as written and no harm can come to you unless you are a case that badly needs an auditor. Good luck in your voyage to YOU.

1

On the State of Man

1

On the State of Man

Man started his journey to present time some countless eons hence. Through blood and slaughter, earthquake and tidal wave, through muck and parching sand, through misery and strivings, grief and happiness he has progressed, generation by generation, into the master of the world and the lord of all kingdoms.

What is the ideal state of this "animal," man? What are his goals? What are his limitations? What is there about him that is good and what is bad?

In the course of his adventures, man made one very important discovery—and it has worried him ever since. He found that he had a mind. He found that he could think. Finally he understood that his mind was his best weapon. And he found that privation[1] and injury or perhaps demons could deprive him of the full use of that weapon—his mind.

Through ages of philosophers, shamans[2] and priests, he has attempted to resolve this primary worry and thus resolve a

---

1. **privation:** lack of the ordinary necessities or comforts of life.

2. **shamans:** (especially among certain tribal peoples) persons who act as intermediaries between the natural and supernatural worlds, using magic to cure illness, foretell the future, control spiritual forces, etc.

primary problem. Man wants to know what there is wrong with his mind, if anything, and he wants to know what might be the ideal state of his mind, if such a state exists.

He has wandered into countless strange bypaths in a quest for answers to these problems. He has seated himself on mountaintops and in caves for whole lifetimes just to ponder the riddle of himself. He has gone to war, he has starved, he has worked and reviled and written just to solve these two mysteries.

And now, as these words are written, his terribly perplexing mind has given birth to an idea and his hands have given form to a weapon which may resolve man forever by destroying all civilization. Thus he *must* solve the two principal mysteries of his mind.

Can the nature of man be changed before the works of man vanish forever under the thud of man's most powerful product, the atom bomb?

Can the nature of man be changed at all?

Indeed, there is nothing more plastic[3] than man's ability to think and believe. At one time or another, in one part of the world or another, man has accepted or believed things wilder than anything contained in philosophic books. His capacity for change is almost unlimited. It is no idle postulate, then, that man's nature, across the whole world, might change entirely in a span of a few years. One has but to study his history to find such shifts of viewpoint and alterations of character. The inertia[4] of

---

3. **plastic:** pliable; impressionable.

4. **inertia:** a tendency to remain in a fixed condition without change; disinclination to move or act.

populaces is a myth. For instance, the coming of St. Paul[5] to Rome, almost two thousand years ago, changed the nature of all Roman slaves with a firelike swiftness. The appearance of a monk in England at the beginning of the millennium just ending altered the insularity of that island in a few months and sent hordes thundering off to the Crusades filled with a piety and zeal which, before his arrival, were markedly absent. And in the last quarter of a century, the idea of collectivism[6] has flooded out from a desperate band of revolutionaries to change the customs and methods of living of nearly a majority of the population of the world.

If man can alter in such numbers, the alteration of an individual would seem to be relatively simple. And so it is. With new knowledge and with many of his past and present problems suddenly resolved, an individual in a few weeks can present a face to his fellows which has markedly changed.

Man is accustomed to change. The severity of his aberration is normally due to a feeling that he must protest against change. For his environment, all down through his evolutionary line, through any lifetime, has changed almost day by day.

Man is successful. That is evident because he is here today after eons of trial and error, good and bad planning. And he is successful because he can change.

The conquest of his environment has been his own engrossing purpose. Each time he has failed to conquer and control his environs, he has made wide changes in form and methods and has again returned into his kingship.

---

5. **Paul, St.:** (died about 67 A.D.) an early Christian missionary who started Christian communities in many countries and wrote most of the epistles in the New Testament.

6. **collectivism:** the political principle of centralized social and economic control, espically of all means of production.

Man does *not* adapt to an environment. He adapts the environment to himself. And in that lies his success. When he fails to adapt the environment, when he lags in his complete control of that environment, he has altered himself or his ideas until he could again change the environment.

Amongst the many things man has done, in his worries about his mind and his state of being, in his effort to control others, is the adoption of slave philosophies. Each person who invents or uses such a philosophy more or less tends to be, himself, exempt from the slavery thus imposed and to hold, by the invention, the force of others nullified. This is a trick of very limited workability, for it leads eventually into the entrapment of the user himself. It is a demonstrable law, not an opinion, that he who would enslave his fellows becomes himself enslaved.

A "therapy" which teaches that man should adapt himself to his environment, rather than adapt the environment to him, is such a slave philosophy and is not workable only because it is quite the reverse from truth.

Each man of the species seeks one way or another to rise superior to all else. In that is his salvation and, in terms of his societies, his downfall.

Attempts at enslavement arise primarily from fear. Fear comes about with the loss of confidence in one's ability to make his way. Thus is posed a world where self-confidence is sought by robbing others of theirs. This cannot succeed in a complex society.

Man's problem today is not new. It is only more urgent of solution. What is wrong, if anything, with his mind? What is his ideal state?

2

An Ideal
State of Being

2

An Ideal State of Being

Before one can determine what is wrong with a state of being, one should have some idea what an ideal state of being might be. In other words, before one can repair, for instance, a radio, one must have some knowledge of what the radio is supposed to do and how well it could play in a good state of repair.

What, it should have been asked a few millennia ago, is an ideal state of being for man? In what state of mind does he best prosper? What is a well man? What is a happy man? What are the goals of man? In what state of mind and body does man live longest and fare best? What does man want to do? What is he trying to do? What is he?

Before one could presume to advance libido theories[1] and prefrontal lobotomies and magic healing crystals, one should have had some idea of the goal of his efforts.

The engineer, in repairing a bridge, has to have some idea of what a bridge is supposed to do, what loads it is supposed to

---

1. **libido theories:** theories like that of Sigmund Freud's which states that all life impulses and behavior are sex-motivated.

carry, how strong it has to be and what might be expected to wreck it again. This is simple reasoning. The engineer does not look at this bridge he is supposed to repair, sigh, say the problem is too complicated, bicker with several other "authorities" on bridges, put some dynamite in the wrong place and blow it up and then wonder why there isn't any bridge left and begin to explain to passers-by that he was called too late, that was all, that bridges aren't much good anyway.

Yet one fears this has been the method of address to the problem of the human mind and body.

To begin a rehabilitation of a human mind and body, one should know something about their optimum state. That would be the beginning of the answer as to how the mind and body could be rehabilitated. Further, it would be the beginning of an answer as to what environment and conditions best favor the human body and the human mind. After that, one could devise means of achieving an optimum condition.

In this new science there are over two hundred axioms which, one to the next, form a logical structure concerning the mind and body, which structure is demonstrated to be workable by the discovery of many new phenomena. This structure also predicts where phenomena might be found—and when one looks to see if the prediction was true, finds that it is. Accomplishments which people are calling miracles come about because of the logic and phenomena of these axioms.

The goal of man here on this earth is apparently *survival*. And by *survival* is meant everything necessary to survival including honor and morals and idealism and other things which make life bearable. A man survives as long as he can in one lifetime, at the highest level he can attain in activity and happiness. When he can no longer attain to some hope of this ideal, he succumbs. And although one is chary[2] of exciting incredulity, the fact is so easily demonstrated in so many ways with such machine-like scientific consistency, it should be known that man apparently dies in body only and gets born to live another day.

The value of death is not small, since without death man would still be algae in the sea; without death man would be forced to live in a body which no longer fitted the environment. Your auditor can show you such an incident as an earlier death unless you are very occluded. Death has lost its sting in this new science and is seen to be rather practical after all.

Physically, on the evolutionary chain, man is attempting a greater and greater control of his environment. The environment does not control a healthy man. He controls the environment. The surroundings of a sick man, a neurotic or insane man, have a tendency to control him. One sees this clearly as one advances, by this new science, into happier states of mind. One's health and ability rise directly as one asserts greater and surer control over his surroundings. Conversely, one asserts better and better control of his surroundings as he becomes healthier and happier.

Thus there is a second goal. Man is evidently surviving to attain a higher and stronger control of the physical universe. The physical universe is composed of matter, energy, space and time. The coined word for the physical universe in this new science is MEST. That is easy to remember because it is composed of the first letter in each of the four words *matter, energy, space* and *time.*

Of course man may have other goals outside of the physical universe, but we note that he is most concerned here on Earth

---

2. **chary:** cautious or careful; wary.

with a conquest of MEST. Naturally he is concerned about his fellows and living organisms in general, for he is in a sort of brotherhood with all life.

Life in general is engaged upon this conquest and man is the highest form of life on Earth. Without this cooperative effort of all life, a conquest of the physical universe or even survival on a barest-necessity basis would be impossible. Man is sufficiently complex as a mechanism that he must live upon lower orders of life which only in their turn can take sunlight and chemicals and evolve complex foods such as proteins.

Now, one hopes that his reader is not engaging upon that trick common to many readers—people often search and recall only items which validate their old ideas. Pick up a book on philosophy which has been read by a reader who underscores with a pencil and one will find that the most utter banalities have been noticed; only things which *agreed* with the old ideas of the reader were noted. One often wonders why such a fellow reads at all.

The data in this new science aren't isolated opinions but a structural whole, and with that whole, one can accomplish an occasional miracle and can almost always effect a marked improvement in an individual. This has never been done before with any consistency, and so one hopes that these data are being studied a little for themselves, not for how well they may agree with old ideas. For they don't agree with old ideas—and old ideas produced unhappiness, starvation, quick death, wars, insane asylums and much other unwanted bric-a-brac. This is not just a plea for understanding. If you want to get better than you ever could have been before, let's try these on for size and wear them until we clearly see their workability. If, after a thorough trial, you find they do not work, then you have every right to discount them. One can say this to you without any fear that you'll discover otherwise—too many miracles have been happening in this new science.

The list of axioms in the back of this book will give you definitions for pain, pleasure, anxiety and other such things in case you are curious. Here we are only treating the ideal state of being in the framework you will need to pursue the exercises in this volume.

The first item in the ideal state is *I am*. Shakespeare was quite correct with his question, "To be or not to be?" When a man is trying to make a decision, that decision breaks down into a matter of choosing one of two courses: to be or not to be. The highest level of the desirable state is *I am*—no doubts of the advisability of being, no qualms about the future. The lowest level on a survival course would be *I am not*. In between we have the doubts and writhing and indecisions of the weary, the angry, the frightened. When a man has made up his mind as to a course, he is only then comfortable. So long as he hangs in a maybe on any decision he is uncomfortable. In any course there are just two decisions possible, to assume a state of being or to assume a state of not-beingness.

Included in these pages is a Tone Scale which is fronted with its own descriptive data. The ideal state of being is to be found across the top of that scale. The states of death or not-beingness are found across the bottom of the scale.

And here we have the matter of gradient scales. Successes are little bits of living. Failures are little bits of death. Like the battle that was lost all for the loss of a horseshoe nail, a small failure can begin a series of failures which end in actual death. Not that death is very important, besides being painful, but that one tends, then, to give a very heavy weight to failures.

The ideal state of being could be said to be wholly successful in all things. This is opposed by being so unsuccessful that one is dead.

The next point in the ideal state of being is *I know*, opposed by *I know not*. Doubts, worries, grinding efforts at study, all these are simply gradients between *I know* and *I know not*. What man does not quiver a trifle when confronted with the unknown?

The next point in an ideal is *serene*. This drops away, and at the bottom rung, having gone downwards through exhilaration, enthusiasm, cheerfulness, antagonism, anger, fear, grief and apathy, is *dead*.

Trust is the ideal point on the scale of *trust–distrust*. The most distrustful one can become is, again, dead.

The ideal point of longevity would be *always* in a perfect body. The bottom of that scale would again be *dead*.

Full responsibility would be an ideal, opposed by *no responsibility* as an undesirable state.

And finally, but not least, there is *cause* and *effect*. The subject of *cause* and *effect* is so important that it will be mentioned several times in the exercises themselves. One's ideal state is to be the *cause*. The least desirable state would be *effect*. The ultimate in being *effect* is death.

Thus we have a brief statement of what an ideal state might be. Only a few of the points have been given but they will serve.

Ideally, one would be fully aware of being and would *be*. That is *I am*. One would be entirely *successful*. One would *know*. One would be *serene*. One would *trust*. One would be in perfect *health* physically. One could assume *full responsibility.* And one would be *cause* without being unwilling to be *cause.*

Of course, it would be not entirely desirable to attain these ultimates since one would then lack for action. But attaining them as nearly as possible would be a desirable condition.

The odd part of it is, when one drops on any one of these things he drops on all the others, so interactive are these portions of life.

This volume and its exercises and auditing[3] seek to assist the individual upwards toward this state of being which one could call ideal. How closely the individual may attain such a state depends largely upon his own willingness to work at the matter rather than the validity of the tenets themselves.

An ideal state of being, it goes without remark, would not include illness and inability to control oneself or one's environment. Control of oneself and one's environment depend upon his attainment toward the ideal state of being.

---

3. **auditing:** the application of Dianetics processes and procedures to someone by a trained auditor. The exact definition of auditing is: The action of asking a person a question (which he can understand and answer), getting an answer to that question and acknowledging him for that answer.

3

The Goals of Man

3

The Goals of Man

The goal of life in the finite universe may be easily and generally defined as an effort to *survive* as long as possible and attain the most desirable state possible in that survival and, in accomplishing this, to conquer the physical universe.

The cycle of survival is conception, growth, attainment, decay, death, conception, growth, attainment, decay, death, over and over again. This is the major cycle.

There is an inner cycle in a lifetime which has to do with emotion or action. This is action, attempt, success, attempt, failure. Happiness down to failure is the emotional cycle. But these are only part cycles. Just as every death begins new life, so does every failure eventually challenge forth new attempt until death itself is reached. Actually, both failure and death alike are transient.[1] They are educational building blocks on a much longer road. Occasionally, however, an individual becomes so overwhelmed that even successive attempts at life decline.

There is undoubtedly a much, much higher goal which prompts this effort to survive and to conquer. There is probably

---

1. **transient:** not lasting, enduring or permanent.

reason above that level. In this new science we are interested in *how* life is surviving, not *why*. Perhaps we know much of *why* right now. Perhaps we will know all of it someday. At the moment it is enough to know *how* life is surviving.

What is embraced in the survival and actions of one man? We see clearly that animal and vegetable efforts are necessary for man's survival. We can see that living is teamwork on the part of all life. How much of this teamwork is included in the activities of one individual?

We have what we call *dynamics*. Dynamics, in life, resemble, somewhat, effort in physics. A dynamic is the urge to survive along a certain course. A dynamic is the persistence in living. It is the effort to live.

Very low on the Tone Scale, in the psychotic[2] or neurotic band, individuals think they survive for themselves alone. This, of course, would not be possible. As one rises up the Tone Scale into better states of being, he expands his sphere of interest and action. But no matter what he thinks in a low-tone state, he is still surviving on the many dynamics, even if in a limited state.

There are eight dynamics. These embrace all the goals of survival an individual has. They embrace all the things for which he survives.

None of these dynamics is more or less important than

2. **psychotic:** an individual who is out of contact to a thorough extent with his present-time environment and who does not compute into the future. He may be an acute psychotic wherein he becomes psychotic for only a few minutes at a time and only occasionally in certain environments (as in rages or apathies) or he may be a chronic psychotic, or in a continual disconnection with the future and present. Psychotics who are dramatically harmful to others are considered dangerous enough to be put away. Psychotics who are harmful on a less dramatic basis are no less harmful to their environment and are no less psychotic.

another. And, oddly enough, when one is blunted or shortened, so blunt or shorten all the rest. When one offends against one, he automatically offends against all the others. These dynamics are very easy to demonstrate.

The **first** dynamic is **self.** This is the effort to survive as an individual, to be an individual. It includes one's own body and one's own mind. It is the effort to attain the highest level of survival for the longest possible time for self.

The **second** dynamic is **sex.** This dynamic has two sections, 2s and 2c. The first section is sex itself, the sexual act, anything relating to the physical action of sex. The second section is the urge for survival through children, the product of sex. This dynamic also includes a portion of family, since the family as a unit affects the rearing of children.

The **third** dynamic is **group.** This is the effort to survive through a group, such as a community, a state, a nation, a social lodge, friends, companies or, in short, any group. One has a definite interest in the survival of a group.

The **fourth** dynamic is **mankind.** This is the effort to survive as a species. It is the interest in the species as such.

The **fifth** dynamic is **life forms.** This is the effort to survive for any and every form of life. It is the interest in life as such.

The **sixth** dynamic is MEST. This is the effort to survive as the physical universe and is the interest in the survival of the physical universe.

The **seventh** dynamic is **life source.** This, in this new science, is separate from the physical universe and is the source of life itself. Thus there is an effort for the survival of life source.

The **eighth** dynamic is **Supreme Being.** This is written with the figure eight turned on its side, meaning infinity: ∞ . It is the postulated[3] ultimate Creator of All and is the effort to survive for the Supreme Being.

When one has a problem which embraces many of the subjects in these dynamics, the optimum solution of that problem lies in benefiting the largest possible number of dynamics. Solutions which injure one dynamic for the benefit of another dynamic result in eventual chaos. However, optimum solutions are almost possible to attain and human thinking seeks at its highest level only to bring the greatest order and the least chaos. At low levels on the Tone Scale an individual will stress one or two dynamics to the expense of the rest and so lives a very disorderly existence and is productive of much chaos for those around him.

The soldier, flinging away his life in battle, is operating on the third dynamic (his company, his nation) at the expense of his first dynamic, the fourth and all the rest. The religionist may live on the eighth, seventh, fifth and fourth at the expense of the first and sixth. The "selfish" person may be living only on the first dynamic, a very chaotic effort.

There is nothing particularly wrong with bad emphasis on these dynamics until such emphasis begins to endanger them broadly, as in the case of a Hitler or a Genghis Khan[4] or the use of atomic fission for destruction. Then all man begins to turn on the destroyers.

The goal of an individual is to be, as much as possible, *cause*

---

3. **postulated:** made a decision to yourself or to others.

4. **Genghis Khan:** (1162–1227) Mongol conqueror of most of Asia and of east Europe to the Dnieper River.

or partner of *cause* on all these dynamics at once without becoming *effect* or partner of *effect* on any of them. He cannot do this completely. But the degree of his success depends upon how closely he can approximate *cause* and how little he can be an *effect* on each.

The whole of *survival* is a dynamic, the only dynamic. But *survive* breaks down into these eight.

Philosophies in the past have laid emphasis on one or another of these dynamics to the exclusion of others and so such philosophies had but limited workability. Psychotherapies have stressed this or that dynamic independent of the others and so did not achieve very great results. Freud, for instance, laid very heavy emphasis on the second dynamic, sex. There is some reason to give this a lion's share in therapy, but only because of the peculiarities of cause and effect and the sexual aberrations of the general culture, not because 2s is more important as an urge or drive than any of the others.

Not one of these dynamics will "drive one mad" when one fails more than another dynamic. But it is quite true that failure or impedance[5] on any one of these dynamics causes impedance on all the rest. Fear on one becomes fear on all. Offense on one becomes offense on all. Success on one is success on all. Defense on one is defense on all.

The proofs of the existence of these dynamics are contained in the workability of the processes which develop from them. It happens that when one thinks of an individual as running wholly on the first dynamic and tries to make a workable therapy on that supposition, the individual does not lose his psychosomatic ills and he does not improve. When one tries to treat the

---

5. **impedance:** something that obstructs or hinders.

---

second dynamic exclusively as a therapy, the individual does not improve. When one uses all these dynamics in resolving his problems, one obtains marked and startling results.

Perhaps the authoritarian will argue that just because a thing works is no reason one should use it. Authoritarians do not achieve any results beyond their own satisfaction—which is not reason enough for the student or technician who wishes to get things done.

The goals of man, then, stem from the single goal of survival through a conquest of the material universe. The success of his survival is measured in terms of the broad survival of all. One man, working hard to save the first dynamic, might short-sightedly destroy all the others. Where then would be the first dynamic?

4

The Human Mind

4

The Human Mind

It is common to think of the human mind as something which just happened in the last generation or so. The mind itself is actually as old as the organism. And according to earlier guesses and proofs established by this new science, the organism—the body—is rather old. It goes back to the first moment of life's appearance on Earth.

First there was a physical universe which happened, we know not how. And then with the cooling planets, there appeared in the seas a speck of living matter. That speck became eventually the complicated but still microscopic monocell. And then, as the eons passed, it became vegetable matter. And then it became jellyfish. And then it became a mollusk[1] and made its transition into crustaceans.[2] And then as a land animal this particular track of life which became man evolved into more and more complex forms, the tarsus,[3] the sloth,[4] the anthropoid[5] and

---

1. **mollusk:** any one of a large group of animals having no backbone, soft bodies not composed of segments, and usually covered with a hard shell of one or more parts. The shell of molluks is secreted by a covering mantle and is formed on snails, clams, oysters, whelks and mussels. Slugs, octopuses and squids have no shell. Mollusks make up a phylum in the animal kingdom.

2. **crustaceans:** animals with a hard shell, jointed body and appendages and gills that live mostly in water. Crabs, lobsters and shrimp are crustaceans.

3. **tarsus:** tarsier: any one of a genus of small, nocturnal primates of Indonesia and the Philippines, with wide eyes and long, bare tails.

---

finally man. There were many intermediate steps.

A very materialistic man, seeing only the material universe, becomes confused and vague about all this. He tries to say that living organisms are simply so much clay, wholly a part of the material universe. He tries to say that after all, it is only the "unending stream of protoplasm," generation to generation by sex, that is important. The very unthinking man is likely to make many mistakes not only about the human mind but the human body.

We discover now that the science of life, like physics, is a study of statics[6] and motion. We find that life itself, the living part of life, has no comparable entity in the physical universe. It isn't just another energy or just an accident. Life is a static which yet has the power of controlling, animating, mobilizing, organizing and destroying matter, energy and space and possibly even time.

Life is a *cause* which acts upon the physical universe as an *effect*. There is overwhelming evidence to support this now. In the physical universe there is no true static. Every apparent static has been discovered to contain motion. But the static of life is evidently a true static. The basic text of axioms of this new science demonstrates this conclusively.

Life began with pure cause, evidently. With the first photon it engaged in handling motion, and by handling motion ever

4. **sloth:** a very slow-moving mammal of South or Central America that lives in trees.

5. **anthropoid:** any tailless ape of the families Pongidae and Hylobatidae, anatomically resembling humans, and comprising the gorillas, chimpanzees, orangutans, gibbons and siamangs.

6. **statics:** things which have no mass, no location and no position in time, and which have no wavelength at all.

afterwards, accumulated the experience and effort contained in a body. Life is a static, the physical universe is motion. The effect upon motion of cause produced the combination which we see as the unity of a live organism. Thought is not motion in space and time. Thought is a static containing an image of motion.

Thus one can say that with its first impingement upon motion, the first thought about the physical universe began. This static, without volume, wavelength, space or time, yet records motion and its effects in space and time.

This is, of course, analogy. But it is a peculiar analogy in that it sweepingly resolves the problems of mind and physical structure.

A mind, then, is not a brain. A brain and the nervous system are simply conduits for physical-universe vibrations. The brain and nerve trunks are much like a switchboard system. And there is a point in the system where the vibrations change into records.

An organism is motivated by continuing, timeless, space-less, motionless *cause.* This cause mirrors or takes impressions of motions. These impressions we call "memories" or more accurately, *facsimiles.*

A *facsimile,* as you know, is a simple word meaning a picture of a thing, a copy of a thing, not the thing itself. Thus, to save confusion and keep this point before us in this new science, we say that the perceptions of the body are "stored" as facsimiles.

Sights, sounds, tastes and all the other perceptions of the body store as facsimiles of the moment the impression was received. The actual energy of the impression is not stored. It is not stored if only because there is insufficient molecular structure in the body to store these energies as such. Physical-universe energy is evidently too gross for such storage. Further, although the cells perish, the memories go on, existing, evidently, forever.

A facsimile of yesterday's hurt toe can be brought back today with the full force of the impact. Everything which occurs around the body, whether it is asleep or awake, is recorded as a facsimile and is stored.

There are facsimiles of anything and everything the body has ever perceived—seen, heard, felt, smelled, tasted, experienced—from the first moment of existence. There are pleasure facsimiles and bored facsimiles, facsimiles of sudden death and quick success, facsimiles of quiet decay and gradual struggle.

Memory usually means recalling data of recent times; thus we use the word *facsimile,* for while it is the whole of which memory is a part, the word *memory* does not embrace all that has been discovered.

One should have a very good idea of what a facsimile is. It is a recording of the motions and situations of the physical universe plus the conclusions of the mind based on earlier facsimiles.

One sees a dog chase a cat. Long after dog and cat are gone one can recall that a dog chased a cat. While the action was taking place one saw the scene, one heard the sounds, one might even smell the dog or cat. As one watched, his own heart was beating, the saline content[7] of his blood was at such and such a point, the weight of one's body and the position of one's joints, the feel of one's clothing, the touch of the air upon the skin—all

---

7. **saline content:** salt content.

these things were recorded in full as well. The total of all this would be a unit facsimile.

Now one could simply recall the fact that one had seen a dog chase a cat. That would be remembering. Or one could concentrate on the matter and if he was in good mental condition could again see the dog and the cat, could hear them, could feel the air on his skin, the position of his joints, the weight of his clothing. He could partially or wholly regain the experience. That is to say, he could partially or wholly bring to his consciousness the "memory," the unit facsimile of a dog chasing a cat.

One does not have to be drugged or hypnotized or have faith in order to do this. People do variations of this recall without any knowledge of this science and suppose that "everybody does it." The person with a good memory is only a person who can regain his facsimiles easily. A little child in school learns, today, by repetition. It isn't necessary. If he gets good grades it is usually because he simply brings back "to mind," which is to say, to his awareness, the facsimile of the page of text on which he is being examined.

As one goes through life he records twenty-four hours a day, asleep and awake, in pain, under anesthetic, happy or sad. These facsimiles are usually recorded with all perceptics, which is to say, with every sense channel. In the person who has a missing sense channel such as deafness, that portion of the facsimile is missing.

A full facsimile is a sort of three-dimensional color picture with sound and smell and all other perceptions plus the conclusions or speculations of the individual.

It was once, many years ago, noticed by a student of the mind that children had this faculty[8] of seeing and hearing in memory what they had actually seen and heard. And it was noted that the ability did not last. No further study was made of the matter and indeed, so obscure were these studies that I did not know about them during the early stages of my own work.

We know a great deal about these facsimiles now—why they are not easily recovered by most people when they grow up, how they change, how the imagination can begin to remanufacture them as in hallucination or dreaming.

Briefly, a person is as aberrated as he is unable to handle his facsimiles. He is as sane as he can handle his facsimiles. He is as ill as he is unable to handle his facsimiles. He is as well as he can handle them.

That portion of this new science which is devoted to the rehabilitation of the mind and body deals with the phenomena of handling these facsimiles.

A person ought to be able to pick up and inspect and lay aside at will any facsimile he has. It is not a goal of this new science to restore full recall perception, it is the goal to rehabilitate the ability of a person to handle his facsimiles.

When a person *cannot* handle his facsimiles, he can pull them into present time and discover himself unable to get rid of them again.

What is psychosomatic illness? Demonstrably, it is the pain contained in a past experience or the physical malfunction of a past experience. The facsimile of that experience gets into

---

8. **faculty:** an ability, natural or acquired, for a particular kind of action.

present time and stays with the person until a shock drops it out of sight again or until it is processed out by this new science. A shock or necessity, however, permits it to come back.

Grief, sorrow, worry, anxiety and any other emotional condition is simply one or more of these facsimiles. A circumstance of death, let us say, causes one to grieve. Then one has a facsimile containing grief. Something causes the individual to bring that facsimile into present time. He is unaware of it, is not inspecting it, but it acts against him nevertheless. Thus he is grieving in present time and does not know why. The reason is the old facsimile. The proof that it is the reason lies in processing. The instant the facsimile is discharged of its painful emotion, the individual recovers. This is processing in one of its phases.

The human mind is only a phase of the continuing mind. The first spark of life which began animating matter upon Earth began recording facsimiles. And it recorded from there on out. It is interesting that the entire file is available to any mind.

In previous investigations I occasionally found facsimiles, which were not hallucination or imagination, which seemed to go back much earlier than the present life of the preclear. Having by then the tool of Effort Processing, it was possible to "turn on" a facsimile with all perceptics at will and so it was possible to examine the earliest periods possible. The genetic[9] blueprint[10] was thus discovered and I was startled to have laid bare, accessible to any future investigator, the facsimiles of the evolutionary line. Many auditors have since accomplished the same results

---

9. **genetic:** by line of protoplasm and by facsimiles and by MEST forms the individual has arrived in the present age from a past beginning. Genetic applies to the protoplasm line of father and mother to child, grown child to new child and so forth.

10. **blueprint:** any pattern or model; template.

and thus the biologist[11] and anthropologist[12] come into possession of a mine of fascinating data.

There are those who know nothing of the mind, and yet who get amply paid for it, who will talk wisely about illusion and delusion. There happen to be exact and precise laws to delusion. An imaginary incident follows certain patterns. An actual incident is entirely unmistakable. There is a standard behavior in a facsimile of an actual experience: It behaves in a certain way; the individual gets the efforts and perceptions with clarity and the content of the incident expands and remains fairly constant on several recountings. An imaginary incident contracts in content ordinarily and the individual seeks to keep up his interest then by embroidering it. Further, it has no constant efforts in it. Those who cannot take time to establish the actuality of facsimiles before becoming wise about "delusion" are themselves possibly quite delusory people.

The human mind, as the present mind of man, differs not at all from the most elementary of minds, that of the monocell, except in the complexity of brain appendage.[13] The human being is using facsimiles to evaluate experience and form conclusions and future plans on how to survive in the best possible manner or how to die and start over again.

The human mind is capable of very complex combinations of facsimiles. Further, it can originate facsimiles on the basis of

---

11. **biologist:** a specialist in biology, the science of life or living matter in all its forms and phenomena, especially with reference to origin, growth, reproduction, structure and behavior.

12. **anthropologist:** one who specializes in anthropology, the science that deals with the origins, physical and cultural development, biological characteristics and social customs and beliefs of humankind.

13. **appendage:** a subordinate part attached to something; an auxiliary part; addition.

---

old facsimiles. Nothing goes wrong with the mind except its abilities to handle facsimiles. Occasionally a mind becomes incapable of using a facsimile as past experience and begins to use it in present time continually as an apology for failure. Then we have aberration and psychosomatic illness. A memory of pain contains pain and can become present-time pain. A memory of emotion contains emotion and can become present-time emotion.

5

The Control Center

5

The Control Center

Every mind may be considered to have a *control center*. This could be called the "awareness of awareness unit" of the mind, or it could be called simply "I."

The control center is *cause*. It directs, through emotional relay systems, the actions of the body and the environment. It is not a physical thing. Here is a diagram of the control center, "I," in relation to the emotions and the body and environment.

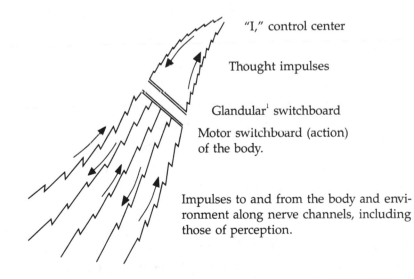

"I," control center

Thought impulses

Glandular[1] switchboard

Motor switchboard (action) of the body.

Impulses to and from the body and environment along nerve channels, including those of perception.

---

1. **glandular:** having to do with glands, any organ or specialized group of cells that separates certain elements from the blood and secretes them in a form for the body to use, as epinephrine, or throw off, as urine or sweat.

The total function of "I" is the estimation of effort. It thinks and plans and resolves the problems of future effort.

When "I" has estimated a needful effort and puts it into action, its impulses impinge against the glandular-system switchboard. The glandular system is a relay unit. It turns the emotional impulse into action.

The motor switchboard is a complex set of physical circuits and these go to various parts of the body and channels of perception in order to coordinate physical action at the direction of the glandular system.

On a return circuit, the environment or the body, through the nerve channels of perception and the channels in the body itself, an impulse from the environment or the body goes into the switchboard and is directly recorded by "I" as a facsimile. The emotional system, in a mind in good condition, is bypassed on an incoming impulse unless "I" directs it expressly into the glandular system.

The physical body is a carbon-oxygen motor. It has been built out of the eons of experience, the summaries and conclusions of "I." Its internal motions and actions can be placed by "I" in the category of "automatic response." Thus the heartbeat and circulatory system are automatic in action. Thus many other motions of the body are automatic. But, as can be demonstrated, any of these motions can be altered by "I."

The glandular system is quite complex as such, but its function is simple. It is the translation medium, evidently, for thought. The system is partially physical and partially thought.

Thought is definitely comparable to nothing in the universe of matter, energy, space or time, having no wavelength, weight, mass or speed and being, therefore, a zero which is an infinity or, in short, a true static. Thought, thinking and life itself are of the same order of being. Demonstrably they have no wavelength, therefore contain neither time nor space. Thought only appears to have time because in it is recorded physical-universe time. There is obviously an "action" in thought but, as obviously, it is not action in this universe. (To see the proofs of this character of thought, see the axiomatic text.)*

Thoughts are these facsimiles which we have been discussing *plus* the *prime thought*, "to be," which can occur at any time.

Now, this subject can be made much more difficult than it is. Thought or the life static acts upon the glandular system to produce physical actions. Physical actions act in the sensory channels (the nerves) to produce thought recordings.

The environment does not control thought. Thought tries to be *cause*. However, the body and the environment have certain needs in this action for the conquest of the physical universe, and so thought, the "I," must give permission to be an *effect*. When it gives permission to be affected, it can then be an effect, and only then can the environment control the body. Thought gives up a sphere of control and that control sphere can be affected thereafter. Here we have what has passed for the stimulus-response mechanism whereby the individual is restimulated or upset or stimulated by the environment.

Facsimiles are filed by *time*. A facsimile from an earlier time is more effective than a later facsimile. If one decides a thing today and decides the reverse tomorrow, today's decision remains active unless cancelled out by being recalled or processed. In the matter of a habit such as smoking, for instance, a young

* *See the Axioms of Dianetics, beginning on page 233. —Editor*

boy, to appear grown, decides to smoke. Twenty years later he decides not to smoke without doing anything about the original decision. Thus, he "can't break the habit," which is to say, he can't overcome an early decision with a later one. He could stop smoking simply by recalling and knocking out the earlier facsimile *to* smoke.

Because of the stress of living, which was no less to the monocell than it is to the modern man, the organism cannot help but become an *effect*. It seeks to remain cause as much as possible. But the mind is running a carbon-oxygen engine called the human body, an engine of narrow tolerance which operates between 95 degrees F. and 106 degrees F. and ordinarily at 98.6 degrees F., which cannot go two miles below the surface of the earth or three miles above it, which has to be fed at least every twenty-four hours and which, because of its early training as a monocell dependent upon sunlight and minerals for its food, needs six to eight hours of sleep every night, and which is capable of just so much physical stress before something breaks.

Further, the method of procreation used by the mammal requires another organism, and thus one must admit to an effect from another being. Further, man developed into a pack hunter, which is to say he was most successful as a group of men, and so had to submit to leadership or the onerous[2] responsibilities of leadership in order to succeed, and thus had to be a further effect.

Fortunately, there is a working rule in the span of all lives that each new generation seems to begin with all old facsimiles submerged and inactive, except for blueprinting the new body and with "I" ready to record experience freshly for this life. As

---

2. **onerous:** burdensome, oppressive or troublesome; causing hardship.

soon as one begins to fail, "I" calls up old facsimiles and starts to use them. And we have trouble mentally and physically.

Without the vast background of past experience, the blueprint of the present body would not exist. A monocell cannot conquer very much physical universe—a man can. Thus, by these cycles of life and death, of starting as cause and becoming effect, the race develops.

The human mind is a natively self-determined computer which poses, observes and resolves problems to accomplish survival. It does its thinking with facsimiles of experience or facsimiles of synthetic experience. It is natively cause. It seeks to be minimally an effect.

It is in its best operating condition when it is most self-determined on all dynamics.

It becomes aberrated when it has desired to be an effect and has lost track of when and why, thus losing control of the facsimiles.

Knowing these things about the human mind, we can resolve its aberrations and its psychosomatic illnesses.

6

Emotion

6

Emotion

As the operating mechanism between thought and action, *emotion* should be well understood.

Emotion exists to monitor motion. Thought itself seems to have an emotional impulse which is free of physical-universe waves. This is studied in various ways, but it is only important to us in the resolution of the problems of the human mind.

Various emotions produce various actions. Anger, for instance, is the catalyst[1] for attack. Fear is the signal to withdraw. Grief is the signal to be quiet and initiate nothing. Apathy is the signal to be dead or feign[2] death so that a marauder[3] will go away. Various glandular compounds are injected into the system to produce these results. Fear and grief, for instance, have an added compound to make the flesh taste bad—for man is but recently a food animal.

There is an entire scale of emotions to produce certain motions. And there is a herd reaction, as witnessed in mass

---

1. **catalyst:** a person or thing which precipitates an event or change.
2. **feign:** make a false show of; pretend; imitate.
3. **marauder:** a person or animal who goes around in search of plunder.

---

hysteria, whereby emotion acts upon others—a mechanism developed in the control of hunting packs whereby the entire pack could feel afraid and run or feel angry and attack without any other command.

This shows up additionally in any modern leadership. The leader is that one who emotionally affects others most strongly toward positive action.

In interpersonal relations, emotion plays an enormous role. In this new science we have what is called *counter-emotion*. Incidents quite often will not reduce until the preclear is made to feel the emotion of others toward him. But quite aside from this manifestation as an ethereal[4] something, there is the real mechanism of sympathy. One person shows grief in order to get support from the other. The other shows sympathy and gives the support. Man is so interdependent and the physical universe so occasionally rigorous that all interpersonal relations are built upon this dependency or its denial.

The broad field of the dynamics indicates the generalized character of emotion.

The test of these conclusions is their workability. You will discover in processing the enormous importance of emotion. The emotion of an individual can be frozen by some facsimile he once wanted but now does not want, and he thereafter handles motion according to that emotion. Thus a person can be chronically angry or chronically in apathy and his behavior on all dynamics is the behavior of that emotion.* By knowing this and

* See the "Tone Scale" in Science of Survival by L. Ron Hubbard.—Editor

---

4. **ethereal:** light, airy or tenuous.

---

the activities of any level on a Tone Scale of emotion, one can predict completely the actions of any given individual or handle him with ease.

The ideal state is fully self-determined emotion. Only then can one be happy and successful.

7

Processing

7

Processing

The effort in processing is devoted to the goal of raising the individual on the Tone Scale. This involves rehabilitating his ability to handle his own facsimiles.

Processing may necessitate the reduction of a number of facsimiles by Thought, Emotion or Effort Processing.

It is a peculiarity of a facsimile that no matter how violent may be the efforts and counter-efforts of its content, no matter how sad or terrible may be the situation it involves, once that facsimile is processed by impressing it against reality several times, it no longer has any power, force, effort or thought content. There are many ways of accomplishing this. In earlier works, cruder and longer methods were used but they accomplished the same purpose.

A memory, a facsimile, contains a record of everything that happened in the actual incident—sight, sound, taste, pain, emotion, efforts of the individual, efforts of the environment against the individual. The individual moves it into present time and keeps it for various reasons and then believes he is unable to rid himself of it. It produces strange compulsions or obsessions or aberrations in general and it can produce, with its efforts, its original physical pain.

A facsimile so held by the individual can make him ill. It can even kill him. Such facsimiles produce over 70 percent of the illness of man and make him weak enough to fall prey to the diseases and accidents which account for the other 30 percent. Sinusitis,[1] arthritis, eye trouble, liver difficulties, ulcers, migraine headaches, polio[2] aftereffects and so on, down the long, long list, surrender if one reduces the facsimile causing the trouble. Whether or not the facsimile is reduced depends to some degree upon the skill of the auditor. For instance, in my first book on this new science, I was guilty of overestimating the ability of my fellow man and have had to work hard since to simplify the techniques and theory so as to make the success of processing much more certain. It is now in the miracle class, so they say. But even now and then, someone is too old or too inaccessible for the skill of the auditor working upon him and so only an alleviation occurs rather than an eradication of the trouble.

The end goal of processing has no finite end. The auditor simply tries to raise his preclear up the scale as far as possible in the time allowed and to eradicate the most evident psychosomatic. There are levels of the Tone Scale which have not been attained but which seem attainable. These unattainable levels—at this time—are so far above anything ever attained by any man before this that the preclear need not worry about being lifted only a little way.

The preclear generally starts with the environment in rather heavy control of him. The modern educational system, various laws and parental authority all seek to cause the preclear to be an effect of the environment rather than a cause of environmental effects. When he has come to a level where he can be self-determined on the majority of the dynamics, his case is considered closed. This book assists him to attain the goal.

1. **sinusitis:** an inflammation of a sinus or the sinuses.

2. **polio:** an acute viral disease, usually affecting children and young adults, caused by any of the three polioviruses, characterized by inflammation of the motor neurons of the brain stem and spirial cord, and resulting in a mortor paralysis, followed by muscular atrophy and often permanent deformities.

8

The First Act

8

The First Act[1]

The processing section of this volume is divided into fifteen Acts. Each one of these covers a certain phase of a case. If the individual is working with an auditor then he will find that the auditor is piloting him through these same fifteen Acts and that this book is being used supplementarily to auditor checking. If the individual has given himself the task of going through this volume by himself, he follows the same procedure and each section is of necessity to be taken up in turn.

Each Act is begun by a description of what the process means and how it is applied and the end it is intended to accomplish.

It is not necessary to *believe* what you find in this volume for the material to work. If you begin processing as in the doubtful class, you will find your doubts resolving as you proceed.

Another can read these processes to you. You can read them yourself. You can do them between sessions with an auditor. You can get an auditor to do all the work for you.

---

1. **Act:** a stage of auditing. Applies solely to the particular process in use at a certain case level.

You will find included a Chart of Attitudes toward life. This might be called a "button chart" for it contains the major difficulties people have. It is also a self-evaluation chart. You can find a level on it where you agree and that is your level of reaction toward life. This chart complements the Hubbard Chart of Human Evaluation but is specially prepared for this volume and for this type of processing. Your use of the chart in your processing is described later.

You will also find a disk included with this book. The disk is employed whenever there is a long list of questions. Its use is described where it is first used in the section.

You may find these processes too difficult for you and would therefore desire some assistance. There are many professional people all over the world qualified in the application of this technology. By writing to the nearest Church of Scientology, using the list of organizations at the back of this book, you can find professional auditing services to assist you.

This new science has moved very rapidly and new developments have cut down the number of hours required in processing to below one hundred with the new techniques. You should count on spending at least a hundred hours with this present book, including any Effort Processing you may receive from an auditor.

This book, by itself, will do more for you than professional processing could have done in June of 1951, much less June of 1950. Into it has gone an additional two years of intensive work and investigation. Anywhere that this text or these processes disagree with books or data earlier than December of 1951, this book, not the earlier work, is correct. The line of advance has been very consistent but sometimes a superficial student cannot follow the logical advance line.

While an individual does not have to understand this new science if he is being audited, one who is working this volume by himself should have a fairly good understanding of basic theory.

It will save time if you will review the text of this volume up to this point and understand it. Then answer the following questions. Write in the book with a pencil.

What is the goal of life?

What is life trying to accomplish?

How many fields is the life organism interested in?

What is a facsimile?

What is the purpose of the human mind?

What is meant by *cause* and *effect*?

Is a facsimile permanent?

How does "memory" or "remembering" differ from reexperiencing facsimiles?

9

The Second Act

9

The Second Act

The anatomy of the static of life demonstrates it to have three interdependent characteristics. Each one of these three is as important as the other two. They are reality, affinity and communication.

Reality itself could be considered that on which man agrees to be real. There is an old, moth-chewed[1] philosophic concern about perception. Are things real only when we see them? Or are things real? In other words, is there *any* reality? Well, desks and chairs seem very real to me. And they seem very real to you. Thus we agree that there are desks and chairs and people and cars and a world and the stars.

Sane men have a very solid agreement on reality. They agree that things are real. Insane people have hallucinations. Hallucinations are imagined realities with which nobody else agrees. When an individual does not agree with the rest of the race upon the reality of matter, energy, space and time, the rest of the race locks him up. Ideas are not matter, energy, space or time and so there can be disagreement on ideas and agreement upon the reality of matter, energy, space and time. This agreement upon

---

1. **moth-chewed:** same as *moth-eaten*: out of fashion; antiquated.

MEST, then, is reality. Reality could be said to be agreement above 2.0 on the Tone Scale, agreement not so much with people but with MEST's actuality. This is one corner of our triangle.

The next corner is affinity. The physical universe has what is known as cohesion.[2] Matter stays together. This is, in the life static as it operates on matter, affinity. Affinity is love above 2.0. *Love,* as a word, has too many meanings, and so we use an old, old word, *affinity,* as meaning the feeling of love or brotherhood from one dynamic to another.

The third corner of the triangle is communication. Communication is actually done via the sense channels. One sees a rock. By sight he is communicating with the rock. He feels a blade of grass. He is then communicating, via a sense channel, with the blade of grass. When one talks to another person he is sending an impulse from "I" to the vocal cords which set up physical-universe sound waves which reach the ears of the other person, are translated into nerve impulses and so convert into an impingement upon "I" of the other person. Communication by talk, then, goes from life to life via the physical universe. It is the same with touch. One person touches another. This is communication via the physical-universe persons. There may be direct, non-physical-universe communication channels from "I" to "I." The most tangible of these is emotional impact.

One cannot have affinity without agreement. One cannot have agreement without some form of communication. One cannot have communication without agreement. One cannot have agreement without affinity. One cannot have communication without affinity. This inevitable triangle may be at any level

---

2. **cohesion:** (physics) the molecular force between particles within a body or substance that acts to unite them.

on the Tone Scale, high or low. If communication is destructive, the affinity drops to anger and agreement is violent disagreement.

At 0.0, which is death, affinity, communication and reality are wholly physical universe for the body and are the cohesions, the connections and the aspects of the physical universe.

At 1.0, which is fear, the affinity is poor, being fearful, the communication is twisted and consists of lies, the reality is poor and is agreed upon for covert purposes.

At 2.0, which is antagonism, the affinity is broken into hostility, the communication is nagging or disagreeable, the reality is contradictory to others just to contradict and is therefore poor.

At 3.0, which is above the normal person, affinity is love, it is present but reserved, the communication is conservative, the reality is cautious but is agreed upon after being proven.

At 4.0, which is cheerfulness, affinity is affectionate, communication is free and constructive, reality is good and agreement is general.

Above 4.0 we have many levels, but ARC (affinity, reality and communication) are getting above a physical-universe aspect. Out of ARC we can derive any understanding. In fact, logic evolves out of ARC. At 4.0 we have lower-level understanding and understanding increases to complete knowledge when a very high band is reached—above 20.0.

A, R, C, are actually the interplays of life active in the physical universe.

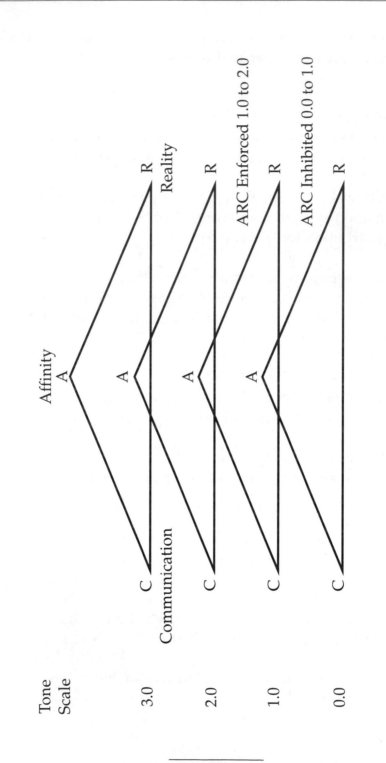

When you communicate with an antagonistic person, you have to enter into an "affinity" and a reality of 2.0. When you show affinity for 1.0, which is fear, you inherit the communication and agreement level of the 1.0. An individual, to escape this inevitable transaction, has to be above 4.0 on the Tone Scale.

In order to have an understanding of yourself, you must have good ARC with yourself.

It is not evil to like yourself or love yourself. It is very low toned not to be fond of yourself.

All the dynamics are interactive. If you love others you will love yourself. If you hate others you will hate yourself. If you hate men, you will hate along the other dynamics even when you cover it with "sympathy," as you will discover in a later Act.

A healthy state of being is to be a friend to yourself. If you have few friends, if you don't like friends, you won't like yourself either.

If you are afraid of people, you won't trust yourself and will be afraid of what you might do.

If you are afraid of animals you will also be afraid of possessions and sex and people and anything else.

Occasionally people have special fears. These are only concentrations upon one thing. A person, without admitting it, will also be afraid on the other dynamics, but will not have recognized it.

It is not enough to suddenly determine to love everybody. That is forcing affinity on yourself.

Affinity is enforced from 2.0 down to near 1.0. Around 1.0

we have "propitiation," buying people off, pretending affection. From here on down affinity is inhibited.

Thus we see that enforced, demanded ARC is aberrative. And we see that inhibited ARC is also aberrative.

Let's put this to test. Do you recall a person you had to kiss? Well, did you feel agreeable toward this person? Did you want to touch (communicate with) or talk to this person?

And another test. Do you recall a person who pushed you away when you felt affectionate? What was your immediate communication reaction? What was your agreement?

And another one. Do you recall a person who demanded that you talk to them? What was your level of affinity? What degree of agreeableness did you feel?

And yet another. Do you recall a person who demanded that you agree with him against your wishes? What was your level of affinity? What was your level of communication?

And still another. Do you recall a person who continually corrected you? This is inhibited agreement. What was your reaction level on affinity? What was your reaction as to communication?

Do you recall a person who was afraid of anything and everything? What was your affinity? What was your agreement?

A person high on the Tone Scale reacts down toward but does not necessarily reach the level of the person he addresses. However, he tends to reach toward that level. And if he stays in the proximity of a lower-toned person long enough he will eventually become chronically in that tone.

Do you know somebody who affects you badly after you have been in his company for a while? Does this person like people? Does he tell the truth? Does he communicate easily? Do you agree with his views? Here is ARC in action in present time.

After you have been in the vicinity of somebody who insists you talk, insists you agree, insists you feel as he feels, what is your own tone level toward him?

After you have associated with a person who won't let you talk, won't agree with you, won't let you feel as you want to feel, what is your reaction? Where is this person on the Tone Scale? This is an inhibited ARC person or below 1.0. This person is afraid or apathetic. This person has endocrine[3] ills. This person lies. This person hides things. This person is physically and mentally maladjusted.

It happens that anyone on a given level of the Tone Scale seeks to pull everyone else to that level of the Tone Scale. A low-level individual is pulled up a bit by a high-level individual and then the high-level individual comes down a bit.

Low-toned people work toward succumb. Below 2.0 the effort is toward death—one way or another, covertly or overtly, toward succumb. The angry person, failing to destroy others, will destroy himself. The apathetic person is almost dead. The activity of persons below 2.0 is directed toward the gaining of sympathy. They try to make higher-toned people sympathetic and thus destroy them. Sympathy for low-toned cases is a social aberration. It is deadly.

No low-toned person can be "helped." Try to help a person

---

3. **endocrine:** pertaining to any of the various glands, as the thyroid, adrenal and pituitary glands, that secrete certain substances or hormones directly into the blood or lymph.

below 2.0 and the result is ingratitude plus, in the end. For the goal of that person is to succumb. Higher-toned individuals don't need help.

Low-toned persons can be audited to above 2.0, however, after which they will seek to survive along all dynamics. If you suppose you lie below 2.0 and have persevered this far, you don't.

There is, by the way, very practical present-time use of this data about ARC. If you want a person to agree with you, address him at his obvious tone level and you will go into communication with him and he will feel affinity for you. If you want affinity from a person, use his methods of communication to others *with* him and go into agreement with him on his concept of the other dynamics. A salesman can sell a 1.5 (anger case) anything if that thing is shown to be destructive to other dynamics.

This is why the government, a rather 1.5 affair, buys atomic fission as a weapon rather than a means to send man to the stars.

Here, then, is the Second Act. First achieve an understanding of the factors in understanding—ARC—contained in this section. Then answer these questions.

List the persons in your present-time environment who enforce affinity on you.

List the persons in your present-time environment who enforce agreement upon you.

List the persons in your present-time environment who demand that you communicate with them.

List the persons in your present-time environment who refuse your affection.

List the persons in your present-time environment who won't let you communicate with them.

List the persons in your present-time environment who refuse to let you agree with them.

Now go back and put a Tone Scale number after each name as an estimate. Where is each one on the chart of triangles earlier in this section?

Don't worry about your accuracy. This is only to give you an estimate of the kind of reaction your environment might have on you and to promote your understanding of these people.

Now take the first person you listed and go to the Chart of Attitudes which accompanies this volume. From the number you assigned the person, go across the big chart at that level. If you assigned somebody to 2.0, follow 2.0 across the big chart. Read each attitude on the 2.0 line horizontally across the chart. This should give you some understanding of that person. And it should tell you what his effect might be on another.

Take the next person with your assigned number across the chart. Follow on through with each person you listed.

You probably duplicated several listings with the same number.

With this exercise complete, let us delve a little into the past.

List persons in the past who *insisted* they were your friends. This is a variety of enforced affection.

List persons in the past who insisted you agree with them.

List persons in the past who insisted you communicate with them.

List persons in the past who would not show you affection.

List persons in the past who refused to communicate with you.

List persons in the past who would not let you agree on things.

Include all your parents and relatives here and as they come into these classifications.

Assign a Tone Scale number to each one.

Check each one for attitudes across the big chart.

What effect do you suppose all these attitudes, past and present, have on you?

10

The Third Act

10

The Third Act

With the help of the Chart of Attitudes let us take a look at your present-day environment.

You may have realized, while inspecting this chart, that you yourself were not quite at the top. You need not worry particularly if you discovered this. Unlike some witch doctors in modern dress, this book is making no effort to condemn you. There were various reasons why you permitted yourself to be lowered on this Tone Scale, for you had to give your permission to have anything serious happen to you (a matter which we will cover under *self-determinism* in a later section of this volume).

Let us make an assessment[1] of how you regard things in your today. Write the answers. (See the chart for the data in each column given.) *Use phrases and words of the chart in your answers. Write the Tone Scale number of the phrases.*

What is your most common emotion?

---

1. **assessment:** an inventory, an examination, a calculation or evaluation of a case.

How do you feel about survival?

How right are you about what you do?

What responsibilities are you willing to shoulder?

How do you feel about possessions?

Do you feel you are anybody?

Do you think most about the past, the present or the future?

How does motion affect you?

How do you handle truth?

Do you trust or distrust?

Do you know or are you doubtful?

Do you want to cause things or be an effect?

What is your "state of beingness" (next to last column)?

Turn back to the Second Act and look over the people you have listed. Do any of your reactions match theirs? In other words, are you comparable to any of those persons listed?

You should be able to discover that you are carrying, in present time, the past attitudes of others. In present time you should be *you*. The phrases you listed in this Third Act actually don't describe *you*. They describe those parts of you which you have turned over to other people in the past. You are carrying on attitudes of people who are probably departed long since. They are not very survival.

A little bit or a great deal of *you* is described up along the 16.0 to 40.0 band of the chart. Our job is to get all of you as high as possible on the chart and leave the parts of "you" which rightly belonged to others behind us.

Human beings, operating along all the dynamics, are actually rather heroic and noble characters. They see cruelty or suffering and they, particularly in their youth and strength, take it on to spare the world. They see someone, even themselves, perform a cruel act or have an unhappy experience, and they regret it. Then they discover that they themselves can fail. They then blame others for their plight. It is a cycle of nobly accepting something and then, to save one's own being, trying to get rid of it in time.

Youth is so high on the chart innately that it accepts the evil of the world with open arms in an effort to make it a better world. Then, staggering under the burden, finding none to share it, they fight to give it away either by being evil or being sick.

This will become much clearer before we have finished here. And you will be a lot higher on the chart.

Let's assess your present time, now.

What phrase on the whole chart best describes your attitude toward life in general right now?

Can you recall a specific instant when somebody else uttered that phrase? Where were you at the time? Outdoors or indoors? Standing or sitting? Can you recall an earlier time you heard it?

When did you first tell yourself that phrase? And don't tell it to yourself again because you are the firmest influence upon you. What you say to you sticks.

Go straight across the list and, column by column, pick out your attitude toward the world in which you are now living. Write these down in the space below.

Now trace each one of these phrases back to the earliest time you heard somebody else use it. Get the exact moment if possible. Get a visio (a view in memory) of the person saying it. Get as many as you can of each phrase and the earliest time it was uttered. *For this, use your disk.* Put the disk over the phrase you wrote and recall the incident with the perception of it called for on the disk or the emotion as requested by the disk.

You can see now that your present time concerns are to some degree the worries and concerns of somebody else in the past.

The value of past experiences lies in the estimation of the future. Past experiences are not nearly as valuable as one might suppose. There is an enormous emphasis on the value of experience. Go to make out an application form for a job and you will find that they are mostly concerned with experience. It is a sort of trap to enslave people, giving their experiences such value.

Actually, a snapping bright mind and an alert body are worth a hundred thousand years of "experience" behind some dusty desk or counter, and an ability to do a "quick study" of a subject is so much more valuable than an education—complete with a hundred A's—in that subject that one might be led to suppose that maybe "education," as it is laughingly called, might possibly be overstressed. Check your history and you will discover that the men whose marble busts adorn the modern halls of learning did not themselves have a formal education: Bacon, Spencer, Voltaire, etc., etc., etc., down the whole list; two or three exceptions prove the rule. Not even long study has as much value as people might have wanted you to believe. Your life, from any instant in it, can be free of all past experience and your carbon-oxygen motor would continue to run and you could pick up what you needed to know in a couple of months, even change your name, and yet survive handsomely. If you won a Nobel prize last year, that's tough: You will try madly to keep the experience and be a Nobel prize winner instead of trying to be enthusiastic enough in the tomorrows to win another prize. The getting is the sport, the having is a defensive action and makes you a platoon pinned down by enemy fire. Thus with experience as with MEST.

So let's look at present time.

And let's be blunt.

What are you trying to hide in present time? What would

happen to you if it were discovered? How many things like this are there in present time?

Don't bother to list them. If other people found these things out they would probably blink, maybe they'd chatter over fences. You might get fired or divorced. But I'll tell you a secret about secrets. No single person to whom you uttered the confidence would *not* have a similar list to hide. They've all masturbated and had clandestine affairs and a lot of them venereal diseases. They've stolen money and maybe some have even left a cold, dead body in a culvert. They've lied and cheated and done blackmail. And the funny part of it is, only those who have a long, long list of things to hide would even begin to reprimand you.

And another thing. Anyone who punished you would someday regret it. A dean in college who threatened to flunk me for writing a bit of truth in what was the longest sentence in the English language (five hundred words without colons or semicolons) had it weigh upon his mind to such an extent that he wrote me, years afterwards, when he had retired and was nearly dead, the most astonishing apology.

You are treating yourself in present time much as you were treated by others in the past. And you punish yourself far more than anyone would ever punish you. The suicide is simply self-executioner, having been found guilty by his own court.

Next, how hard and to whom are you trying to be *right* in the face of anything and everything including facts?

What responsibilities are you shirking? Why?

What are you doing with your possessions? Why?

What do you think of yourself? Why?

Is the future or the past receiving your most intense thought? Why?

Do you flinch at motions? Why?

How closely do you stay to truth in present time? Why not?

Do you trust your environment? Why not?

What don't you *know?* Why not?

What are you trying to cause? Why?

What are you trying to make affect you? Why?

Who are you trying to blame in present time? Why?

What are you blaming yourself for in present time? Why?

Do you like your work? Why?

Is your sex life satisfactory? Why?

What threatens your present security? Why?

Self-confidence alone is security. Your ability is your security. There is no security but you. Let's make the best possible you we know how. Almost all the things you thought of in the above list can be remedied by your own action without consulting for a moment the permission of anything or anyone. Innately, deep down, you know this. Actually, you are a giant tied down with cotton lint. You tied the knots and furnished the string and said where you'd lie. The only trouble you might have in processing is refusing for some strange but discoverable reason, having to do with concern for others, to burst these light strands and stand up. Fortunately this volume offers more than such inspiration, but the cold, basic truth is that you are a vital and necessary part of this world and anything that is wrong with you, you have assumed in an effort to be what has passed for "human."

11

The Fourth Act

11

The Fourth Act

You will note on the edge of the Chart of Attitudes that from 0.0 to 1.5 is considered to be severely aberrated; that from 1.5 to 2.8 is considered to be neurotic; that from 2.8 to 10.0 is considered acceptable.

When these figures were first calculated, it was thought that normal was about 2.8. It isn't. That is generous beyond generosity. Normal is well below that, according to amassed data since the first computations. The reason for this seems to be in two distinct fields. The first is the environment, the second is education.

Education, continued long enough in the usual school and college, depresses the individual toward 0.3 or apathy. The person being "educated" is, day after day, immobilized, made into an effect by instructors and denied original thought. He becomes a habitual "effect" and ceases to cause. He begins to respond automatically according to a pattern of manners given him by the home and the school system. This is the primary reason why the modern college has yet to turn out an artist from an arts major. An artist must be a cause and continue to be cause. Majoring in writing, for instance, is a sure route to being an editor, or worse, a critic, rather than a writer. All the editors and critics, according to writers, are failed writers. They are also arts majors for the most part, with wonderful grades. The writers revolted early. This is no criticism of modern education or educators, it is a small signpost pointing toward the source of low tone.

Education is also done in the home. The level of that education is the level of the home. The goal of most parents is obedience. Obedience is apathy. Most *bad* children become good the moment you let them up the Tone Scale.

The general society today may be commented upon by a review of the front pages of the newspapers. The "public" buys the news it wants. The newspapers, being an expanded version today of the old house-to-house advertising handout, print news to sell papers. The tone range of the usual front page today is from 1.5 down to 0.1. A man could invent something that would feed all the starving people in the world with ease and get a news notice one inch high near the obituary column. The blood-soaked and sordid[1] front pages of the world's newspapers tell you that man has sunk pretty far down. His newspaper is the modern American's Roman Circus, his government is becoming his corn.[2] Bluntly, the normal is a very sick man.

There are three valid therapies. The first is processing. The second is education. The third is environment. We find the first two in this new science. The third must sometimes be changed, for a preclear may be in such a vigorously painful environment that his gains in processing are lost in his struggle against his surroundings. Very fast processing is one answer to the environmental problem. Wives have been known to practically murder

---

1. **sordid:** degraded.

2. **corn:** referring to the practice of ancient Rome of feeding people and providing official public amusement (circuses in the arena) in order to prevent unrest. Also known as "bread and circuses."

husbands who dared try to get up out of apathy via process-ing. Apathy is a very docile and obedient, if sick, state of not-beingness. Husbands have been known to react similarly when their wives tried to get well. And in the past some mental practitioners have gone raving insane when one of their patients started to climb into well-being via processing.

The chief difference between the severely aberrated, the neurotic and the "acceptable" bands is concerned with *time*.

The severely aberrated gives his attention mainly to the past. The neurotic is giving his attention mainly to the immedi-ate present. The "acceptable" is giving his attention to the future.

By forcing attention into the present (raising necessity level) one can raise a severely aberrated person into a neurotic level. The AAs do this with alcoholics, persuading them to live for the present only. Your alcoholic, of course, is still trying to untangle the past, with a forgetter known as alcohol, just as your drug addict is shutting off the agony of yesterday with an anesthetic.

However, almost anyone is giving more attention than nec-essary to the past, reserves his living in the present and restrains his planning for the future. Your 1.5, for instance, considers it bad taste to be enthusiastic about the future. "Don't hope too much." For the 0.5, both present and future are unthinkables.

Attention is a remarkable thing in that it must be at opti-mum sweep for a person to be happy. When attention is too fixed on one thing, if that thing is a survival threat, it tends to remain fixed. If a threat to survival is understood to be present and yet cannot be located, attention swings endlessly without fixing. This is "fear of the unknown." Fixed and unfixed atten-tion, when given to dangerous problems, tend to remain that way unless the problem is solved.

The human mind's basic purpose in operation is the posing and resolving of problems it observes as related to survival along any of the dynamics. A problem is resolved when it is answered *yes* or *no*. A problem such as "Should I go?" must be answered yes or no if the mind is to file it as a conclusion. If it continues as *maybe,* the problem stays in the computer and influences the next solutions. Did you ever know a person who had a lot of trouble reaching decisions? Recall a specific time? Well, somewhere in that person's past was a problem which was not answered yes or no but only maybe. A very "serious" sort of a problem comes up with "Was it my fault?" When that one lands on maybe, the computer tends to jam. (The answer, by the way, is that nothing is anybody's fault.)

Problems do not solve for two reasons: The first is lack of data; the second is an earlier unsolved problem on the same subject.

One has to evaluate data in order to resolve problems. When one fixes his attention on something dangerous he is probably overevaluating the data. When one is unable to fix his attention, it is because he cannot find data to evaluate.

This will become clearer to you when you have completed the following exercise. Do it with your pencil.

List five problems, with people or objects or circumstances, which you are not solving in the present.

1.

2.

3.

4.

5.

Now list what you wish you knew about each one of the problems above. (The missing data you wish you had.)

1.

2.

3.

4.

5.

Now list how important you now feel these problems actually are or whether or not they are now solved.

1.

2.

3.

4.

5.

If any of the five problems remain unsolved, list what you would have to do to solve them.

1.

2.

3.

4.

5.

Now let us take a glance at the past. There are several problems, undoubtedly, which you feel you did not solve.

List five problems, with people or objects or circumstances, which you feel you did not solve in the past.

1.

2.

3.

4.

5.

Now list what you wish you had known about each one of the problems above.

1.

2.

3.

4.

5.

Now list how important these problems actually are to your present circumstances.

1.

2.

3.

4.

5.

If any of the above problems still bother you, what would you have to do or know in order to resolve them?

1.

2.

3.

4.

5.

Let us now take a look at the problems of the future.

List five problems, with people or objects or circumstances, which you think you will have to solve in the future.

1.

2.

3.

4.

5.

Now list what you will have to do now to solve these problems in the future.

1.

2.

3.

4.

5.

Now list how vital these problems may become to your existence.

1.

2.

3.

4.

5.

If any of the above problems worry you, it is because you have not decided upon your course of action. Try to list your course as it will probably be taken.

1.

2.

3.

4.

5.

In this same Act, we should take up goals. Some poet once said that a man's dreams were important and that when the last of a man's dreams were dead, dead was the man. He didn't know about this new science.

Dreams, goals, ambitions—these are the stuff man uses for fuel. Survival is nothing but the effort to accomplish action. There is the broad goal of all survival. There is the small goal of a good action. Survival, action and goals are inseparable.

Happiness could be defined as the emotion of progress toward desirable goals. There is an instant of contemplation of the last goal in which one is content. But contentment becomes boredom immediately that new goals do not come to view. There is no more unhappy thing than a man who has accomplished all his ends in life. Gibbon,[3] for instance, died immediately after finishing his great work. It is doubtful if men die when they have great goals ahead of them, save perhaps in the violent action of some attempted attainments. It is doubtful if it would take more than a flick with a feather to kill somebody who has no goals. The Filipino irregular[4] of 1901, battling for an independent state, would charge seventy-five yards and kill his man *after* that man had put a Krag-Jorgenson[5] bullet through the *heart* of the Filipino. A neurotic without goals catches a harmless bug, sneezes and dies. Or sneezes and dies without a bug getting near him.

People always begin with goals. They often fail. When they have failed often enough they stop thinking about the future and

3. **Gibbon:** Edward Gibbon (1737–94) English historian whose chief work was *The History of the Decline and Fall of the Roman Empire.*

4. **irregular:** a soldier or combatant not of a regular military force, such as a guerrilla or "freedom fighter."

5. **Krag-Jorgenson:** Norwegian-designed rifle used by US forces at the turn of the century.

start worrying over the present. When the present hands them a few failures they start worrying about the past. They go "out of present time." If you were simply to walk through an insane asylum and tell each inmate, "Come up to present time," a small percentage would immediately become sane and stay sane. The order would unfix their attention from a past maybe or fix their attention on the present. It has been tried and has succeeded.

More happily, let's examine your goals and fears.

In this column, list five goals you had in the past.	In this column, list what happened to the five goals in the past.
1.	1.
2.	2.
3.	3.
4.	4.
5.	5.

In this column, list five fears you had in the past.	In this column, list what happened to the five fears in the past.
1.	1.
2.	2.
3.	3.
4.	4.
5.	5.

In this column, list five goals which should have been accomplished in your present, now.	In this column, list five goals which you would like to set into the future.
1.	1.
2.	2.
3.	3.
4.	4.
5.	5.

In this column, list five fears which you have in your present.	In this column, list five fears which you might expect to encounter in the future.
1.	1.
2.	2.
3.	3.
4.	4.
5.	5.

Now go back over your lists and for each item in the goals columns, see if you can find some person in your past or present who might have these goals or who might have had them. Some person other than yourself.

Now go down the past and present and future fears columns and see if you can find some person in your past who might have had these fears other than yourself.

When you have noted down these people or one person, answer the following:

Is that person dead? Are those people dead? Did they fail?

You should be able to sort out your own goals from "dead men's goals." And you should be able to sort out your own fears from "dead men's fears."

It's a "very peculiar thing" that you may be seeking a life continuation and life realization from people no longer amongst us in that precise identity.

Out of nobility and grief, so does one take on the burdens of those who have laid down their burdens. This includes pets.

There may be one dead person or half a dozen. One dead pet or two or three. List briefly the goals of each dead person you have loved. Then briefly list the goals of each pet.

You may have wept doing this. If so, come up to present time. Now recall the last good time you had in the fullest detail. Be very precise in trying to reexperience this good time.

Better?

Let's see now if you can recall the following for each person and pet you may have listed.

1. The precise moment you first decided you had affection for them. Any moment you decided you had affection for them.

2. Any moment you decided you were like them. The first moment you decided you were like them.

3. Any time you regretted something you had done to them. The first time you regretted something you had done to them.

4. Any time you felt sympathy for them. The first time you felt sympathy for them.

Do this for each person you listed, each pet you listed.

Now go over the same process again, even if you hit the same incidents.

Go over the same process a third time for each person.

Go over the process a fourth time for each person.

Go over the process a fifth time for each person.

Go over the process a sixth time for each person.

Go over the process a seventh time for each person.

Now take a sweep through all the work you have been doing in this Act. Do that again. Call it concluded.

12

The Fifth Act

12

The Fifth Act

Your Physical Ailments

(If you have found that this processing is a trifle strenuous for you up to this point, it is advised that you give yourself some "Validation MEST Processing." This is contained in another volume.* But if you are only mildly in a state of collapse, continue. It gets easier from here on.)

So far we have been dealing mainly with the processes of thought. It is time we took up physical function and malfunction.

Once upon a time this was a rather serious subject. Two hundred years ago a medical doctor had to be able to sort the bones of the human body by touch only, blindfolded. Less ancient than that, the most fascinating theories existed concerning physical function. A doctor let out a pint or a quart of blood and that cured everything, even life. Recently endocrinologists[1]

---

* Self Analysis *by L. Ron Hubbard. —Editor*

---

1. **endocrinologists:** specialists in the field of endocrinology, the branch of biology that deals with the anatomy and function of the endocrine glands, such as the thyroid, adrenal and pituitary glands, which secrete certain substances or hormones directly into the blood or lymph.

had to study for years to discover an occasionally effective method of handling glands. But in all this time, no effective method of treating physical function existed. A rare remission[2] of symptoms kept medicine at work and eating. Surgery began to be resorted to in a vigorous but unsuccessful revenge for being unable to resolve physical ills.

The main reason this new science had such a dreadful time proceeding into the medical realm with its effectiveness was a tradition, built out of thousands of years of experience, that exactly nothing could be done for the human body except per-haps taking foreign matter out of it and sewing it up when it was gashed and strapping a bone when it was broken. The resilience[3] of the body itself was responsible for the recoveries. "Magic drugs" such as penicillin depend upon the ability of the body, not the drug.

With this much background of failure, the world has been in apathy about the body. It was born, it grew, it died. Surgery and drugs could stem the tide of time a brief moment. But that was all. This dramatic struggle for knowledge of the human body was a struggle against time. Time's scythe in the hands of that grim gentleman, Death, won every contest.

Now and then a mystic would rise in the world and with a few passes of the hand cause the crippled, the sightless, the faltering to bloom with life once more. Then the mystic, the adept,[4] the master would vanish and man would struggle on with attention to their relics but without many repetitions of the miracles.

---

2. **remission:** a relatively prolonged lessening or disappearance of the symptoms of a disease.

3. **resilience:** ability to recover readily from illness, depression, adversity or the like.

4. **adept:** a skilled or proficient person; expert.

That faith or thought could do such astonishing things in the hands of a master or adept brought men like Freud into heavy ambition to resolve the human body's ills by resolving the ills of the mind. The medical profession of his day ostracized[6] Freud. Today psychoanalysis and psychologists speak with contempt of Freud—perhaps they owe him too much. But Freud is the grand old man of psychosomatic healing. He popularized the idea that something could be done about human unhappiness via treatment of the mind and that human ills might be handled by handling the "ego," the "id" and the other mental entities Freud thought he had discovered.

Freud had many pupils—Jung, Adler and others—who decided only they themselves could see the light and so went sailing off into further and further incredibles. Of all these it now seems evident that Freud himself was the only one of them who had even started toward the straight and narrow road to complete physical rehabilitation of the body via the human mind.

In my boyhood I studied Freud secondhand. His brilliant student, the late Commander Thompson of the U.S. Navy, had just left Freud and Vienna when he saw fit to dazzle a young mind with the idea that perhaps the riddle of thought could be resolved. Studying Freud tenthhand, through his books and what people thought people had said about what Freud said, the psychoanalysis and psychiatric world had broken cleanly with Freud years before I even came to a university. There was no studying Freud in any college. They did not teach Freud. He had been abandoned by the professional cliques.

In the meanwhile a new subject had risen in the world. Nuclear physics, they call it now—"atomic and molecular

---

6. **ostracized:** excluded, by general consent, from society, friendship, conversation, privileges, etc.

phenomena," they called it then. No atoms had been split effectively, but from Newton[7] to Halley[8] to Einstein,[9] men had been studying the physical universe and had now encoded the subjects of matter, energy, space and time. Here was a new field of knowledge. It was so new that those of us who studied in it were known as the "Buck Rogers boys," a comic-strip character of the day who sailed off to Mars or Venus and had incredible adventures. We experimented with rockets and the Doppler effect[10] and later found employment difficult to achieve except as orthodox[11] engineers.

Although it was my father's ambition that I become one of these orthodox engineers, bless him, I found that with all this new knowledge, transits[12] were dull. In order to pursue studies in this field I had to write for any magazine that would buy. Many of us, in the decade of the thirties, were "Buck Rogers boys" in earnest, writing "science fiction" for a growing audience of fans. Then came Hiroshima, and "Buck Rogers boys" started to have such importance to the governments of the world that they are almost prisoners.

Having escaped offered employment by Russia and the United States, I continued my work in the field where I had

---

7. **Newton:** Isaac Newton (1642–1727), English mathematician and natural philosopher, formulator of the laws of gravity and motion.

8. **Halley:** Edmund Halley (1656–1742), English astronomer. Best known for his study of comets.

9. **Einstein:** Albert Einstein (1879–1955), German physicist, US citizen from 1940, formulator of the theory of relativity.

10. **Doppler effect:** the shift in frequency of acoustic or electromagnetic radiation emitted by a source moving relative to the observer as seen by the observer: the shift is to higher frequencies when the source approaches and to lower frequencies when it recedes.

11. **orthodox:** customary or conventional, as a means or method; established.

12. **transits:** instruments used in surveying to measure horizontal and vertical angles.

started, the human mind, from the viewpoint of mathematics and nuclear physics. As late as 1950 I was still acting fast to keep out of U.S. Government research laboratories.

Culmination of research in what is popularly known as this new science and more correctly known as Scientology has yet to occur.* But in 1948 a thesis was written and submitted to the medical professions, which demonstrated the workability of alleviating physical ills by an address to mental problems. Much as in the case of the grand old man of mental technology, Freud, the medical profession at first went all-out in ignoring the work and then flew into print to blast it. But the new science had taken root. Tens of thousands of people were working in it. Millions knew about it.

Based on the background of thousands of years of mystic accumulation concerning the mind, Freud's effort to apply his knowledge to the medical concepts of the human body had not resulted in very startling results. But this same background knowledge, filtered through what was now known about the physical universe as in nuclear physics, did produce a uniformity of result comparable to engineering.

The occasional and spectacular effects of the masters in performing miracles could be repeated at will. For where there is occasional effect, according to engineering theory, natural laws exist which can make the occasionalness into predictable results.

New principles in mathematics had to be discovered to make it possible for one to address the mind and rid the body of physical ills. One such principle is that zero and infinity are equal. The qualities of a true static had to be delineated for the first time. Mathematics itself had to be defined. The quality and

---

* *In the years since this book was written, L. Ron Hubbard completed his research into the mind and spirit of man, developing and refining the first truly workable technology for improving the quality of life.* —*Editor*

character of time had to be examined and the definitions improved. All this has taken me about twenty years. The current ability of the result makes it possible for mental aberration and psychosomatic ills to be treated with greater invariability in each passing year. It is doubtful at this time if cases exist which will not resolve by the processes of this new science which yet retain sufficient life and physical completeness to be gotten into communication by an auditor.

One of the most respected commentators on world affairs has paid me the compliment of saying that these developments would probably be regarded in the future as the most significant progress of this century. Another has said that they rank with the three most important discoveries of man. However this may be, a good auditor can now do miracles with the workmanlike precision of an engineer building bridges. There are scores of people alive today who would not be alive except for this new science. There are children and old people who would not be walking except for this new science. Polio ravages, arthritis and scores of other ills are handled daily by this new science with success. If the grand old man, Freud, were alive today, he would probably be cracking his heels in glee. He was amongst the first who supposed that it could be done with complete precision.

I have given you this short history so that you will have a background on what may happen to you. You are not the first. You are about a hundred thousand cases from the first, for although it made its public debut less than two years ago, more people are in process in this new science than are being worked by psychology, psychoanalysis and psychiatry combined. It even works on me: It cost me my retirement from the navy as a disabled officer of World War II—because I was no longer disabled after processing. Further responsibility is mine in the unthinking attitude toward this new science, for I did not properly estimate, a couple of years back, the ability of the average auditor. Thus I oversold the subject in my first book, for I based it only on my own ability to handle the techniques. It required a year and a half to refine these techniques to a point where the average auditor could handle them. This present volume, by the way, is a guarantee that he does.

Your body has a dual composition which is yet a unity. You, without life animation, are only so much physical universe—atoms, molecules in space and time, complex compounds and so forth. That part of you is MEST. The other part of you is what we call the "life static," the thought, soul, vital part of you which animates this MEST, the body. Disconnect the static and you are no longer an animated organism. Funeral processions are given these bits of MEST which are no longer animated by the static. This MEST portion of you is a carbon-oxygen motor. It ceases to be a motor when it can no longer function as a motor, when it is damaged or decayed. When this happens, the animating force, the static, could be said to withdraw support. Then the body becomes so much physical universe—97 cents worth, by old-time chemical costs.

You as a personal identity are the composite of all your experience *plus* an initial decision *to be* and occasional decisions *not to be*. You do not die as an identity or a personality or an individual. You and the MEST body "separate" and the MEST body gets a funeral. You then link into the protoplasm line with your genetic blueprint—the plans of construction of a new body in the orthodox manner of conception, birth and growth. You depend upon some inherent abilities of protoplasm but you, as experience and identity, monitor that protoplasm's ability and modify it. There is a family line, then, from generation to generation, modified by you as experience. You are not necessarily part of that family line. Every child, for instance, distrusts his identity as a family member. And there are numerous cases of record wherein a child, up to the age of three or five, recalled entirely who he had been—but forgot it under the pummeling of his "imagination" by adults. Perhaps you take off after some lifetime and go to heaven. Nobody can argue successfully about that. But you are the source of yourself with regard to various generations.

Now this, by Effort Processing, becomes so irrefutable, so clear and unmistakable, that if it can be disproven, then the laws of heat and fission can be disproven as well. We are on solid ground about immortality and all the rest of it for the first time in history.

You are evidently quite eternal as a personal identity. You get snarled up in the modern social aberrations about only living once and play the game as though you would never get another chance—which you will get as certainly as the sun will rise tomorrow.

Now, if you can handle a body in construction, you can certainly modify one in growth and form. And so you do. You can modify it to the degree of going blind or getting arthritis and being bedridden or having migraines or putting any other imperfection on yourself. You, as cause, are continually shouldering the ills of the world and modifying yourself accordingly.

Once having taken on such an ill to "help" another, you may be very reluctant to give up the infirmity. Evidently it doesn't help the other very much but you, with your social aberration that a person lives only once and never again, take the illness or demise of another very seriously. Much too seriously. And so there you are with somebody's arthritis. Of course, it isn't his. It's an old injury of your own—your own facsimile—which you are holding in place for him. People will give up any illness or infirmity which is theirs—their very own—with immediate ease and no qualms. But they are quite tenacious of the ills they have shouldered for others. This caused old workers in the field of the mind to suppose that people simply refused to get well. No, people simply refuse to give up the illness of others for whom they have made themselves responsible until they clearly see that holding the illness will not bring back or restore the health of that other. It's a wonderful world. Man has condemned man for selfishness for eons and here we find man only gets lastingly crippled or lame to "help" another.

Once it was said that if people knew the world was going to end tomorrow, the communication lines of the world would be jammed with calls from people seeking to say they loved one another. It is probably quite true.

In the field of illness, however, once one realizes how little it helps, one can give up another's aches and pains and resume his own health. It is quite a decision but one which processing itself assists. You may find that you will be trying to make that decision. The other day a totally blind man under processing stopped the session on the abrupt realization that he would see wholly and clearly for the first time in years. Just an instant before his sight turned on, he balked. Why? His trouble with sight had to do with the death of his brother. His brother had been injured and was blinded in an automobile accident. The moment the brother died, this preclear had taken on the burdens of his brother. And he held to them to the degree of total blindness for years.

The auditor had processed the case a little too swiftly. All the emotion of love for his brother was still on the case. Although it obviously would not help the brother—who is probably some-body else now, some happy kid in school—this blind man yet carried that blindness. He is now, at this writing, struggling with his conscience about regaining his sight. He will decide in favor of it—they always do eventually. And it will not hurt or assist the

MEST body of his brother, buried these many years. But the action of this blind man, snatching at his brother's life, trying to get his brother to live when death itself was graying the flesh, remains today as a facsimile containing such a powerful impulse, an impulse great enough to deny sight, that the blind man has to consult long with it before he will give it up.

Your most serious troubles, then, from a physical standpoint, apparently stem from moments when you tried to help and failed. What was done wholly to you, you will be able to bear and discard without hesitation. You might have to consult with yourself a little while to decide to give up your effort to shoulder the burdens of the world. You will give them up, but you'll think about it.

First you had to agree to be so disabled, mentally or physically. Then you had to shoulder another's travail to really get yourself into a secondhand condition. Apparently the very insane themselves, to say nothing of the neurotic, are the very noble characters. They'll stand up to electric shock, prefrontal lobotomies, psychiatry and any brand of torture before they will surrender the facsimiles they are holding for others—and even then they don't give them up! Processed by this new science, the ties which bound them into this self-sacrificing difficulty surrender rather easily.

In view of the fact that you have a lot of margin physically and mentally, we should be able to do the job rather quickly and easily. And you can go out with a clean slate and shoulder some more burdens, which you will. But you'll be in much better condition to do it even if you are what passes for normal now.

Thus, let us take an assay of the MEST you are using just now for a body.

First, answer this question honestly. Would you like to be in better physical condition than at present?

If the answer is "no," you are still trying to help. Even if the answer is "yes," you are still trying to help, but you probably don't realize it.

People usually fail when they try to help. Check over the number of people you have tried to assist in your lifetime. What is the level of gratitude on a long-term basis?

The times you aided somebody successfully aided you. But when you tried to help and failed, the repercussion was bad on you. Thus we want the moments you tried to help and failed. The most flagrant of these, of course, is the case of people who died. You tried to bring them back to life. They died and you supposed you had failed. And later on you failed some more and then you found yourself with an imperfect physique, and calmness a stranger to you.

A little child will try to keep a pet from dying or a grandfather from dying and "blame" himself ever after with the psychosomatic illness of that death.

Who have you tried to help? They're elsewhere now and doing fine. You didn't fail. So let's get you straightened out.

You've made an effort along every single dynamic and every part of every dynamic including your own body and its parts. And you may have been very successful a lot of the time. The failures are what kicked back at you. Well, you can have a clean slate and go out and fight again and be successful again. More people need help than those you have helped. We can have a pretty fine world here if we clean up the slate of yesterday and use that slate to write all over tomorrow. We're in a rut of yesterday when all around us are the suffering of others in today and tomorrow. So let's go.

Let's make a summary of your present body.

List ten things which you would like to have happen to your present body: ten specific conditions of physical being which you wish you could attain in the tomorrows, such as physical beauty or strength, whether you think you can attain them or not. Get as wild as you like.

1.

2.

3.

4.

5.

6.

7.

8.

9.

10.

Now let's be critical. List five things which you think may be wrong with your present physical being. List them with the thought that they might be remedied. Such things as frequent colds, etc.

1.

2.

3.

4.

5.

Now list the persons or pets who have failed or are dead who had things wrong with them. There may be more than one with each. Take the first error you listed above as number one and write the name of the person who might have had that ill after number one below and so on. You may not be able to account for some of the conditions. That is all right.

1.

2.

3.

4.

5.

Now take the illnesses you have attributed to others and, by just memory, try to find a time when that person who had the illness before you demonstrated it or said he had it.

Recall when illness number one was seen or heard by you to be the possession of person number one or the persons you listed under number one.

Take the second ill or malfunction. Recall when person number one was seen to have it or was heard by you to have it.

Continue this process.

Now go all through the list again and recall all the incidents again and see if you can find new moments on the same subject.

Now recall when you first decided you liked person number one. Go on through the list, recalling decisions to like or be like the people you listed.

Recall now a time when you wanted to be like each person you listed.

Now recall times when you decided to help the people you listed.

Recall many incidents where you tried to help these listed people or pets.

Recall times now when you realized you had failed to help these people. For in this last extremity you might have taken on their ills for them.

Recall any time when you felt you were powerless to help anyone. Why did you arrive at such a decision? What were the circumstances of it?

Go over the entire list above step by step again, but now try to get an actual sight or sound of the moment you are recalling.

With this completed, recall doing this particular Act in detail two or three times.

Do not count on your illnesses being gone with this Act. They might have vanished and if so they will stay that way. But if they are, any of them, still with you, there are many more Acts in this book.

13

The Sixth Act

13

The Sixth Act

The subjects of effort and counter-effort, emotion and counter-emotion are very new in the knowledge of man. In continuous investigation of mental and physical phenomena, I chanced upon these manifestations and put them to work immediately. Such was their reach and significance that auditors from coast to coast, within sixty days, were "cracking cases" which they had found hitherto "uncrackable." Thus you can see that it is well to know something about them.

Let us take *effort*. Your mind is continuously at work estimating efforts. When you go to open a door, your mind estimates the effort necessary to turn the knob and, via emotion, puts that effort into action. It estimates the effort necessary to pull the door back and puts that into action. If the door handle turned as desired and the door opened as desired, your estimation of effort was correct.

Your mind calculates efforts for the present and for the future. It puts efforts into action now or in the future. Or it simply estimates them and holds them back and never applies them. Your mind estimates the efforts of the environment, how fast cars go, how hard teacups have to fall to break. And it even estimates efforts when it "daydreams," which is to say that it thinks of the efforts involved in that and that, without even desiring to, puts them into action. Thinking of a goal is putting something into the future to which one can build by effort. An attained goal is a summation of efforts.

If you calculated the door properly, you opened it smoothly. If you calculated wrong and the door stuck, you were wrong. Did you ever have a door or a drawer stick on you consistently? After a while you became angry with it. Then you began to avoid it. For the mind which survives well estimates efforts well. It is *right*, which is to say, it estimates efforts rightly.

The author writing a story estimates many, many efforts. If he is right, it is an interesting story and sells. If he is wrong, it is not an interesting story and it doesn't sell.

The mind all through evolution was subjected to countless efforts on the part of the environment. The wind, sea, sun and other organisms all had efforts to throw at the organism. The organism that handled these *counter-efforts* well, survived well. It came to use these very counter-efforts as its own efforts. The evolution of efforts is from counter-effort to employed effort.

Effort means force and direction. Your life is a contest between your own efforts and environmental efforts.

Any psychosomatic illness you have is some counter-effort, some past effort of the environment, you aren't handling or using right. The facsimile of the effort itself is in the facsimile. Facsimiles are recordings of effort. Perception is the recording of physical-universe efforts and your thoughts, conclusions and efforts about them as well as your emotion.

Effort Processing is easily done. One finds where the fac- simile of an effort is against the preclear and gets the preclear's effort against it. A pain or pressure turns on and, by constant reexperiencing, turns off. But Effort Processing is something which should be done by any auditor and although it can be done by a preclear on himself, must be thoroughly understood by that preclear. There is not enough data in this volume to permit a preclear to Effort Process himself. To do that he would have to study the main body of this science, preferably at the Foundation Auditor's School, or at least through the basic texts.

Emotion and counter-emotion are something else. The preclear should be able to handle these.

You know what your own emotion is: anger, fear, grief, apathy. You have experienced these things. They are part of facsimiles now. Grief is very important as a blocker in one's life. Grief takes place where one recognizes his loss and failure, as in the death of somebody he loved and tried to help.

A facsimile which contains chiefly emotion is called, in this science, a *secondary engram*. This would be a unit of time, ten minutes, a day, a week, wherein one was under heavy stress of misemotion—anger, fear, grief.

The way one runs out such a secondary is simple. It is easier to have an auditor do it for you because you are likely to bolt from it. If you start a secondary you ought to finish it all the way.

No single Act of processing is more beneficial to a case than running out a grief secondary.

If you have nerve enough, this is the way you can do it: You begin with the first moment of news of loss or failure and you run it through again and again, releasing its misemotion simply by reexperiencing it. You do this until long after you think it is gone.

You reexperience a facsimile by seeing it, hearing it, feeling everything in it, including especially your own thoughts and conclusions, just as though you were there again.

A death is done this way: You pick up the instant, the very first instant, you heard or knew anything bad about that event. You contact who gave you the news or how you got it. You go through the whole thing, over and over and over, reliving every portion of it. You reexperience the misemotion. You finally get that facsimile to a point where it no longer has any "charge" in it. Then you run it until it is practically erased.

You will find, as you run it, that more and more detail appears in it.

The danger of running it is that you may lose your nerve and leave it half finished. Don't. Take yourself in hand and run it until it is fully knocked out, so that you could even laugh about it. Don't fake it. Do it.

You can best get started on one by recalling and refeeling earlier times when you loved the person or animal or possession and dwell on this emotion until the loss or death facsimile turns up. If the facsimile eludes you, then get more times when you loved or felt sympathy for the person, animal or object. If it still eludes you, just recall the mean things you did to it, your neglect for it and the thought that if you had been better and hadn't been so mean, it would be well now. Think of the way you tried to help the person, animal or thing. Think of how you failed. Think of your love. And run the facsimile.

Better be in a quiet place where you won't be interrupted when you do this.

You may be an emotional wreck for days. But you'll come

out of it when you've run it all and your level of recovery will be, even to you, fantastic. Your very physical appearance can change for the better on the running of such secondaries.

If you find the whole period is blank and black, recall the times when you promised yourself you would not grieve about it anymore, or the times when you would not give it up.

Then run the times you blamed yourself or others for the incident. And recall the times you regretted things about it.

A man, almost dying, ran two secondaries by himself with this technique and recovered. A woman who had been branded psychotic ran a number of secondaries on herself, knowing this technique, and became a lot saner than her family. A woman whose husband had been dead for ten days had assumed the character of an old woman; her entire glandular system was interrupted. She ran out the secondary of his death in nine exhausting hours, and twenty-four hours later, although she had built her whole life around this man, she looked young and was happy again.

It not only can be done but it is being done. Simply crying about the matter in present time—without reexperiencing it— serves no purpose. The grief has to come by reexperiencing every moment of the secondary facsimile itself. It's rough but it can be done!

A secondary may be a little more difficult because to fear is to flee. So when you get the facsimile around you to run it, part of it says to flee and you may obey it. The way to get around this is to "run" the times when people wouldn't let you get away when you wanted to run.

You can not only bring a secondary or any facsimile up

around you, you can also put them aside, throw them back into time. Halfway through running one this may seem difficult. The thing to do is to flatten it. Then you can throw it away with ease. They are flattened simply by reexperiencing them and getting your old conclusions out of them.

A word of caution. Don't try to run yourself around somebody who may be even faintly critical. And don't argue with somebody about it. The wife, mother, father, the husband, may get into a terrible dither about your effort to feel stronger. They may even have an interest in keeping you down so they can "take better care of you." Run one of these secondaries around such a person and you'll really fix yourself up.

And by the way, be very suspicious of somebody who doesn't think you ought to indulge in this new science. Auditors are always running into situations where they have a son or a daughter in good condition and well on the road to recovery when the parents step in and with every argument in the book, with every "good intention" knock the poor preclear into limbo again. Such people want the preclear under control and instinctively realize that the preclear is getting very independent. The preclear who argues back simply gets himself snarled up again. Best to be calm and do your work in private. Then when you are nine feet tall, do your arguing.

And don't plead with a wife or a husband or a friend to study this new science against his or her will and use it on you. They will manage one way or another to turn the processes around and wreck you. You may have an impulse to use your facsimiles to get sympathy from such a person. It is quicker and easier just to blow out your brains. The result will be the same. For when you force somebody to "help you" and "be sympathetic" who has an interest in keeping you sick, they will manage to make you sick in earnest. Out of their good knowledge and intentions, of course. There is, for instance, a very sick woman who could be straightened out by an auditor in about fifteen hours. Yet her husband, hovering like a mother hen, is violent about letting her be helped: He knows nothing of this new science except that it is successful. She has had three unsuccessful operations for her condition. He is seeing to it that she is going to get a fourth which will probably kill her. These are desires to help — out of a frame of reference which doesn't work. "Keep him calm. Operate on him. Control him. Mama knows best" are the sources of the attitude.

Further, you have always had and use what is known as a *service facsimile*. Every time you fail, you pick up this facsimile and become sick or sadly noble. It's your explanation to yourself and the world as to how and why you failed. It once got sympathy. Sympathy will turn it on again. It may contain the basic condition of being which is now passing for a common cold or sinusitis or a game leg.[1] You fail at something, then you use the facsimile. And you get sympathy from somebody. Well, heaven help you if you are around somebody who doesn't get the line signals. You use the facsimile and then they don't sympathize. You use the facsimile harder. And they are still stone cold. Then you really turn it on. Maybe it was measles that founded this facsimile. Maybe it was when you broke your leg. Well, you'll use it to a point where you'll get all the symptoms again if you don't get sympathy for it. You have two choices: Run out this service facsimile and the reasons for its use as per the remainder of these Acts, or get yourself a new associate or partner. For that service facsimile will get you by and by. You didn't believe it yourself the first time you decided to use it. Then the use of it became automatic. And now you "wonder what caused it." You did.

We remark on the service facsimile at this place, not to have

---

1. **game leg:** lame or injured leg.

it run in this Act, but to acquaint you with its existence. For you may hit it in running a secondary and be very loath to part with it. It is simply a time when you tried to do something and were hurt or failed and got sympathy for it. Then afterwards, when you were hurt or failed and wanted an explanation, you used it. And if you didn't succeed in getting sympathy for it, you used it so hard it became a psychosomatic illness.

Let's take a summary of your body. Maybe we can discover what you are using for a service facsimile. Everybody has one or more than one.

List anything which gets wrong or is wrong with the following named portions of the body, as a repeated infirmity or pain or malfunction.

The head:

The eyes:

The ears:

The nose:

The neck:

The teeth:

The chest:

The lungs:

The hands:

The skin:

The arms:

The shoulders:

The spine:

The rectum:

The genitals:

The abdomen:

The legs:

The feet:

The nails:

The internal organs:

How do you recognize any one particular illness out of these symptoms? Measles? Whooping cough?[2] Getting born? An accident?

Write what you think it might be:

What age did this occur?

---

2. **whooping cough:** an infectious disease, usually of children, that causes fits of coughing that end with a loud, gasping sound (whoop).

Who was present?

What had you failed about?

What failures since have turned these on?

Who doesn't sympathize with them?

Who did?

What is the similarity between the person who did and the person who didn't or doesn't?

What are the differences between the person who did sympathize and the persons who didn't or don't?

Who did you blame?

Who do you blame?

Having and using a service facsimile does not make you a hypochondriac. It simply makes you human.

The facsimile might release[3] right here. If it doesn't, there's a lot of book left.

One word of caution about all this. Process yourself at specific times, not all the time. Choose a processing time and use it. Then when it is over, wait until the next time. Don't go around self-auditing.

In the pictures you get of old incidents, you may be seeing yourself "outside of yourself," not seeing the scene as you saw it then. This is being "out of valence." Simply move in valence to run the incident. Running it outside yourself won't do very much for you. But if you run it very many times, you'll be inside yourself in the scene.

Being outside oneself is the cause of "self-auditing." In an operation or somewhere, you slid out. When you self-audit, you may be in the role of somebody who hurt you (a counter-effort) and you'll just keep on hurting yourself. The section on counter-emotion, later, clears up this condition if it begins.

---

3. **release:** (verb) the act of taking the perceptions or effort or effectiveness out a of heavy facsimile, or have the preclear's hold on the facsimile taken away.

14

The Seventh Act

14

The Seventh Act

Have you been a left-hander who is now a right-hander?

About 50 percent of the human race is natively southpaw but have been "educated" to be right-handers.

As you know, the control center of the left side of the mind-brain system runs the right side of the body, and the right side of the mind-brain system runs the left side of the body. This is a perfect governmental system. It ought to be employed in this atomic age: You take the government of Russia and put it in the United States and you take the government of the United States and put it in Russia. And then you'd have no war.

Thus the mind solved the difficulties of the double control center condition which began about the time man's forebears— you, too—began to emerge from the sea or shortly before.

One of these control centers is the "genetic" boss. It is stronger than the other control center. A natural right-hander is running on his left control center and it is natively the most powerful control center of the body. In such a case the opposite control center is obedient to the chief control center and all is well, coordination is good and no confusions result.

Take a natural left-hander, however, who is running on his right control center and insist that he change to his right hand and you force him to become controlled by his sub–control center. You invalidate his more powerful control center. This causes him to go down the Tone Scale and it causes poor physical coordination between left and right hands.

Did anyone in your family complain that this had happened to him or her? Do you recall that it happened to you?

It has been known for a long while that forcing a left-hander to be right-handed was bad but none knew why and there was no remedy for it.

Further, a control center, confronted with a major failure in life, will abdicate, so to speak, and let the sub–control center take over. Then perhaps it fails markedly and the old failed center takes over. This switching centers can continue and repeat, each time with less power and security of control.

You see evidences of this in strokes and migraines where half the body gets ill. The control center, having failed often already, takes over again. It takes over suddenly. If it is already rather disorganized with past failures, its reign is marked with physical failures, particularly for that side of the body.

Thus this Act is addressed not simply to left-handers who became right-handers by education but to anyone, for the shifting of alternate centers can happen to anybody and usually does.

The way the old center is rehabilitated, or the way both centers are rehabilitated, is rather simple. One picks up the times of shift. These are marked by moments of major failure or the sudden recollection of a past situation, the recollection being strong enough to cause the shift. Center A is in control. Something in living suddenly recalls to Center B that it was once successful and a shift will occur. Or Center A will have a failure and Center B is left holding control. Or a charge is run off the case and an old center is relieved of its burden of failure and takes over.

In processing you may run into these shifts. A shift may be followed by intense exhilaration. This, however, may fade out in a day or two. That doesn't mean that it will never come back. It means a temporary shift of centers took place.

The ideal condition is to relieve both centers.

The childhood is normally occluded in people, before mise-motion or physical-pain incidents are discharged. This occurs by a shift of centers. The child starts out in good condition but in childhood is handled so heroically[1] that he fails on his native center. The other center then takes over. This shifting occludes the experience, to some degree, of the old center. Thus, early education, parents, pets may be occluded. As you pry them into view you are actually rehabilitating an old center.

You should know this so that you will not be alarmed on several counts. The first is temporary "euphoria" where you stay happy for two or three days and then get sad again. That's a temporary shift, evidently. The second is physical unbalance which can occur as a temporary affair, where you get a toothache or a headache on one side and the other side seems numb. Another is a shift of interests.

You won't contract amnesia, but this shift of centers may be

---

1. **heroically:** in an extreme manner.

responsible for amnesia. A sudden shift of centers occludes present time experience and then may shift back. It doesn't happen in processing.

There is also a whole set of "pseudocenters," the personalities of people whom you've tried to help and have failed. These are "valences." A person can have two or ten dozen of these "valences," can be one personality to Joe and another to Agnes, can change at a certain period of life into an "entirely new person." This is simply a manifestation of the life continuation manifestation discussed earlier. All these are relieved by getting rid of misemotion.

The ideal state of affairs is the attainment of a supercenter. Right and left centers are always subcenters. A "supercenter" is acquired on discharging all the sympathy and regret on a case or, in short, the misemotion.

Think this over carefully. The incidents are marked by sudden changes in physical health, old illnesses disappearing, new illnesses appearing. Falling in love may shift centers. A bump on the head may shift them. Any emotional shock might do it. In particular, incidents which diminish one's concept of his ability to handle his surroundings and people may shift centers. A sudden drop, because of an experience, of one's importance, may shift centers.

A death, a severe loss, a realization of one's unimportance, may shift these centers. Each incident listed should be run. If it is difficult to run as a facsimile, wait until later in the volume when you have learned how to chain-scan yourself and then refer back to this list. If possible, use the technique for secondaries as of the Sixth Act to accomplish the purpose.

Write down the number of times, with approximate dates, when you might have shifted centers.

Write down, briefly, the shock or loss which might have occasioned these shifts.

15

The Eighth Act

15

The Eighth Act

Done by yourself, without an auditor's assistance, you may find this processing rather heavy for you, and again you may not, depending on how much life endowment[1] you have.

But here is a technique which is relatively simple. It does things for you quickly. In the fall of 1951 I developed this technique from one called Chain Scanning, an effort to run pain in wholesale quantities from a case, which did not work. This is Lock Scanning. It does work.

Take your pencil and draw a line, a vertical line, on the space to the right. Make the line about five inches high.

Now, at the bottom of this line, mark it *conception*.

An inch above the bottom, draw a horizontal line and mark it *birth*.

At the top of the line, mark it *present time*.

Now, just above birth, draw a **very** heavy horizontal bar about an inch long.

At intervals of every quarter or half an inch, irregularly, above the heavy bar, draw a light line horizontally, half an inch long. There should be a dozen or two of these light lines.

Now mark the heavy horizontal bar *painful incident*.

Now mark the light bars above it, each one, *lock*.

---

1. **endowment:** a gift of nature.

151

Here is a picture of a *time track*. That is the long vertical line. It is a way to plot your facsimiles, experiences in life, against time. Actually these facsimiles can be sorted around at will by you. But stretching them all out this way, they can be conceived as a track of time through which you have lived.

Now, during this lifetime, on this time track, various things happened to you. Some were good and some were bad. Up to your teens you had the big goal of growth and after that you had other goals.

This track is a continuous facsimile. But it is made up of a lot of facsimiles, particular experiences which either stand out or remain hidden.

Painful incident is any incident which was painful: a death, an operation, a big failure, big enough to render you unconscious, such as an accident. You've had many of these but we are graphing just one to show you what happens to any of them.

Locks occur when you decide that the environment is similar to the painful incident. Locks occur when an individual is tired or has had a minor failure in life which reminds him, perhaps, of the major failure.

The technique known as Lock Scanning starts off from an early lock of the painful incident but not the painful incident itself. One doesn't pay any attention to that: it is more or less inflated by the locks and can be handled as an incident just like any other facsimile, which is to say, put aside at will. But sometimes the locks have to be cared for before the painful incident slips away. Of course the painful incident itself can be run by Effort Processing, but that's pretty heavy to do by yourself. Further, these locks have to be scanned anyway.

A lock, then, can be treated by Lock Scanning.

To lock-scan, one contacts an early lock on the track and goes rapidly or slowly through all such similar incidents straight to present time. One does this many times and the whole chain of locks becomes ineffective in influencing one.

Now more work with the pencil: Number the locks. Mark the first one above painful incident, 1, the next 2, and so on.

When you start to lock-scan, you will find an incident of the type required. You will scan yourself through all such similar incidents to present time. Maybe the earliest one you found on this scan was lock 8 and you scanned from there through the remaining locks to present time.

On your next scan, try to find an earlier lock. The first scan made an earlier one accessible to you. This new start may be lock 5. Scan from lock 5 to present time through all similar incidents.

On your next scan you may find an even earlier lock. Scan from there to present time through all similar incidents.

You do this scanning on any one chain until you are "extroverted" about it, which is to say, until you find yourself in present time thinking about something else, your tone probably up.

If you continue to lock-scan after you have "extroverted" you will "drop through" into another chain on some other subject. This isn't bad, but you want to stop scanning when you are extroverted. One more scan will find you scanning another chain.

It can happen that during scanning you hit what is known as a "boil-off." This means that you become groggy and seem to go to sleep. This is evidently caused by old unconsciousness coming off. It hasn't much benefit and apparently occurs when two facsimiles conflict with each other. Actually you could lock-scan yourself into a great deal of "boil-off." You could probably spend five hundred hours lock-scanning this and that and boiling off. That's the slow road. The object of Lock Scanning is not boil-off. Boil-off means too many secondaries, too much grief and too much regret. If you find yourself boiling off too much (a little is quite in order) run regret and blame as in a later section.

This technique has to be known and understood if your processing is to go swiftly.

To show you what happens, here's some work with an eraser: Take the graph you made. Run your eraser from lock 7 to present time. Some of the lines lightened. Now run the eraser from lock 5 to present time. Now from lock 1 to present time. Now pass the eraser from 1 up many times until the lines are almost erased. That is what happens to the facsimiles you lock-scan.

It is possible for you to "hang up" in Lock Scanning. You start to run a chain of incidents and find yourself "stuck" half-way to present time. Don't flounder around or get alarmed. You've hit a *postulate*, a decision you have made not to get rid of something or never to get over that incident. You've hit something you yourself thought which keeps you from going on by the incident. Possibly it is regret. Feel the feeling of regret and you may become unstuck. Or feel the feeling of blaming you or somebody else for the incident. Or simply feel the counter-emotion, which will be covered in a moment and is a ripe subject for scanning. It's expected you'll finish reading all this before you try it.

You can lock-scan at various speeds. You can scan so fast you don't even know what the incidents are. That's *maximum*.

Or you can scan so slowly that you know every word said. That's *verbal*. Or you can scan speeds in between. You may have been living with somebody who insisted you hear every word they said and you may find yourself scanning at a speed which might, facetiously,[2] be called "turtle." That is too slow. Most scanning is done at *accelerated*, which simply gives one a glimpse and concept of each successive incident.

Light emotion, counter-emotion, blame, phrases, people, anything can be scanned.

One of the most important things to scan is *counter-emotion*, which was mentioned but not explained in Act Seven.

Have you ever walked into a room and known that people had been talking about you or fighting just before your entrance? The "atmosphere" seems charged. When somebody stands and bawls you out, do you feel the anger?

You have emotion which you discharge at people. You try to make them enthusiastic or make them see the seriousness of something or you show them your contempt. Well, they sense it not so much as words but as emotion.

A good orator is one who can throw out a great deal of emotion and so thrill or energize an audience. The same thing could be done with misemotion, anger, grief, etc.

Mass hysteria is a well-known phenomena. One person in a crowd is panicky. The whole crowd becomes panicky without even knowing what is wrong. This is a built-up manifestation of "herd instinct." Man traveled in packs. It was safer to run or to

---

2. **facetiously:** in a manner not meant to be taken seriously or literally.

charge instantly than it was to dawdle around for verbal orders. Thus, mass emotion. This is a survival instinct.

More than that, emotion is the relay between thought and action. Emotion is the glue in facsimiles.

There is *thought, emotion* and *effort*. Thought is one fringe of emotion. Effort or physical action is the other fringe of emotion.

Efforts and counter-efforts have been mentioned. Somebody hits you. That is a counter-effort. You resist the blow. That is the effort. You use two kinds of effort, the effort to remain at rest and the effort to remain in motion. There are two counter-efforts which you can experience. One which moves against you and one which refuses to move. You can see this very easily. Right now you are making a tiny effort to hold up this book while the counter-effort of gravity is pulling it down. Every day the counter-effort of gravity makes a person shrink during his waking hours, about three-quarters of an inch. At night he gains it back.

Emotion and counter-emotion are similar to effort and counter-effort. You have two goals with emotion. Thought, via emotion, seeks to stop action, self or exterior. Thought, via emotion, seeks to start action, self or exterior. Anger, for instance, seeks to stop exterior action. Fear seeks to start self-action to get away.

Now, emotion is emotion whether it is yours or another's. Live around a person who is continually angry and you will begin to emotionally react toward that anger, for the anger seeks to stop you whatever you do. Live around a person who is afraid and you will pick up their fear and try to counteract it with emotion of your own, usually seeking to stop their flight. Or you can get into the unhappy state of duplicating their counter-emotion with your emotion. You do this whenever you agree with somebody. (The chief hole in light books which seek to win friends and influence people. They also make people ill eventually because of agreement on emotion.) Agree with an angry man and you'll get angry too. Agree with an afraid man and you'll get afraid. Agree with a man in grief and you'll feel your own grief, and so on, as covered in ARC in an earlier Act.

You can feel your own emotion and the counter-emotion when examining a facsimile. Or you can feel simply your own emotion. Or you can feel the counter-emotion only. You can take what you want out of a facsimile. The trick is to take what is essentially aberrative out of it.

Now let's see what happens to a counter-effort. This, let us say, is that pressure you sometimes feel in your stomach. That's just a facsimile of an old blow but it is sometimes very uncomfortable. How do we get rid of that facsimile? Well, we can lock-scan all the times it ever bothered you. And we can lock-scan it until it won't bother you again. That's one way. It's around a lot, so we can run it as a service facsimile by effort (or an auditor can run it, which is best when effort is in question). Or we can run a grief charge off Grandfather's death, Grandfather having had a stomach that bothered him. Or we can run off the counter-emotion. We have a dozen dozen ways to handle that stomach trouble.

Let's see how the fastest way works. That may be counter-emotion scanning.

If it's a pressure or a pain, it is a facsimile of some pain that happened before and which still exists "in memory" as a facsimile. Obviously it eludes our control of it or it wouldn't hurt. What makes it elude our own control of it? Well, after the blow was struck or whatever the counter-effort was, somebody in the environment began to throw emotion at that very spot. That is counter-emotion to you. The counter-emotion took over that facsimile of the counter-effort and it is being held there by somebody else's counter-emotion. That's the way the pressure or pain in the stomach may add up.

Don't let's try to get complicated about this. It's simple. George has been hit in the stomach by a baseball. Later his mother is sympathetic. That makes it a "good facsimile," so George holds on to it. Then one day he gets married. His wife, a 1.5, begins to nag him about eating. She gets angry at him. He wants sympathy instead so he holds up this facsimile for sympathy and it doesn't work. Her counter-emotion, anger, alters the baseball-in-the-stomach somatic and puts anger on it. Now George doesn't control it anymore. It is controlled by his wife and her counter-emotion of anger. In processing, George starts to run his wife's anger. This old baseball facsimile turns on strongly and then goes away, never to return.

Where the emotion of others is concerned, an ache or a pain is fair game. But oddly enough, one has to have loved or felt sympathy for another in order for that person's counter-emotion to have much effect.

The cycle is then as follows: a blow or a pain becomes a facsimile. Facsimile is used by individual. Or isn't handled well by him. Somebody close to him gets angry at him or fearful or sad. That emotion (counter-emotion) turns on the old blow or pain. If the counter-emotion is heavy, not even Effort Processing can touch that old facsimile until the counter-emotion is removed from it.

The process is this: You have an ache or a pain. You can't get rid of it simply by identifying its source or other light means. You locate a time when somebody you loved threw counter-emotion at that particular spot. You scan, by Lock Scanning, all the counter-emotion thrown at that spot, whether it was sympathy or anger or fear. It doesn't matter what you do about your own emotion.

One of two things will happen: You will find the old facsimile and throw it away or you will find counter-emotion from a great many people, run that off by scanning, and then discover a big secondary which will have to be run or a painful incident which has to be run by Effort Processing and is the service facsimile.

Whatever happens, you won't go wrong by running any and all counter-emotion you can find.

Every atmosphere in which you have lived has an "emotional quality." You will find that emotion doesn't come from humans only. You will find times in your life when you ran away from an atmosphere alone, not for any other reason than that you did not like the "feel" of it. You will find you have avoided people, certain persons, certain groups, because you did not like the counter-emotion. You may discover that that vague blur which you recalled as your education was thrust out of sight just because you hated the school atmosphere, its counter-emotion.

Primarily and foremost, you will find counter-emotion sitting around by tar-bucketsful whenever you failed. This is a mixture of counter-emotion and your own emotion or regret and blame.

Counter-emotion has been thrown at you, your thoughts, specific parts of your body and, in particular, that great or slight infirmity which you carry around.

Don't be alarmed if, in scanning counter-emotion, some chronic pain begins to turn up like a five-alarm fire. Don't run for a water bucket. Just run more counter-emotion. It's doubtful if it will kill you, for you see, you didn't die before when you actually experienced it.

These are just facsimiles. If the real thing didn't ruin you, the facsimile probably can't. If you have a very weak heart, however, or some such infirmity which means razor-edge between life and death, *use memory only from present time, don't lock-scan, on counter-emotion.* In two years these processes in the hands of the public, an often careless public, have never lost a preclear by reason of a weak heart or some such hair-trigger infirmity, but I must state that that doesn't mean it can't occur. See a doctor and an auditor but don't let the doctor talk you out of the auditor. Doctors always tell people with weak hearts to slow down. That's what's wrong with the individual—he's too slow already.

The assignment of the Eighth Act is first a thorough study of Lock Scanning. Then a thorough study of counter-emotion. Then, finally, testing out Lock Scanning and counter-emotion separately and then as one process. Do the following practice exercises:

Lock-scan everything you have ever heard about this science, good and bad, until you extrovert on the subject.

Lock-scan everything you have ever heard or read about L. Ron Hubbard, good or bad, until you extrovert on the subject. If you haven't heard anything—fine.

Lock-scan every conclusion or postulate you may have made about the science and every decision about it.

If you have ever been audited before by old Standard Procedure,[3] lock-scan all sessions of that auditing.

---

3. **Standard Procedure:** a set of exact steps used by an auditor in auditing a preclear.

If you have ever been audited before, pick up every time you agreed to contact an incident.

If you have ever asked to be audited, lock-scan every time you asked somebody to audit you.

When you have completed this, do this further exercise:

If you have ever been audited, lock-scan the counter-emotion of your auditor and the environment. Get the way his emotion might have felt to you. If you haven't any contact on it, don't worry. You didn't like him.

Pick up somebody in your life of whom you were fond. Lock-scan all the times when you were sympathetic to him or her. But concentrate with your scanning on the emotion from that person when he was in trouble or in pain. Scan until you extrovert on the subject.

Lock-scan through all the times you have tried to help people in minor ways. Do it in general without any attention to counter-emotion.

Now lock-scan through all the counter-emotion of people you have tried to help. Their emotion towards you before and after the aid or offer was extended.

These are exercises. The last action, however, is a very effective process. Now follow with these effective processes:

Go to the Second Act (ARC) where you made a list of people who enforced and inhibited affinity, communication and reality on you. Lock-scan the counter-emotion of these people of the present and of the past in every incident of enforced and inhibited ARC. Check off each name written in the Second Act. Scan until you extrovert on each one.

When you have completed everything to this point, and in particular, the scanning of all people mentioned in the Second Act, continue with the following:

On page 85, in the Third Act, you listed your attitudes toward the world in which you are living. Lock-scan each and every time you made a decision or felt the attitude listed. Take each phrase you wrote and scan every time you felt that way. Then go to the next phrase.

When you have finished this scanning, scan off the counter-emotion in all such incidents.

When you have completed counter-emotion in every incident recalled around your attitude, go to the big chart.

Start at the bottom phrase of column one of the big chart. Scan every time you felt that way toward the world, toward yourself, toward groups, toward animals, toward the Supreme Being.

This process at first glance may appear long. It would only become long if you began to boil off. Probably from twenty-five to fifty hours should be spent on it. They would probably comprise the most profitable twenty-five to fifty hours you ever did spend in terms of an understanding of yourself and the world.

You may strike *secondaries* in this scanning, where fear or grief or anger are heavy. If so, run that incident through as per the earlier instructions in handling secondaries, reexperiencing them over and over until they are discharged. You may be rather occluded, in which case do your best on concepts of incidents. Not all the phrases may apply, although at one time or another in a person's life he decides that his attitude lies in most of these phrases.

It may also be that you will go through various general tone changes. You will strike, in the general run of this processing, a shift upwards on the Tone Scale. You may go through periods of being angry at one person or another or the world at large. Don't sound off too strongly. The action you take because of restimulated anger will only have to be undone later.

(In this process most but not all phrases may have been applied.)

Take the next higher phrase in column one and scan for all dynamics.

Take the next higher phrase in column one and scan for all dynamics.

Progress all the way to the top of column one, scanning each line for each dynamic.

Start at the bottom of column two and take the lowest phrase. Scan each time you told yourself or the world this phrase. Scan for every dynamic.

Take the next higher phrase in column two and scan for each dynamic.

Continue on up column two, scanning each phrase in turn for each dynamic.

Scan each phrase from bottom to top in every column for every dynamic until you have scanned every phrase on the big chart.

16

The Ninth Act

16

The Ninth Act

In this Act we handle emotion and counter-emotion with even more understanding.

The technical background of this is a simplicity, but it is a simplicity which took twenty years to discover. All things are complex when they are poorly understood. The evolution of knowledge is toward simplicity, not complexity. An evolution toward complexity is an evolution toward authoritarianism and pomposity—"You couldn't possibly understand this, therefore I, who pretend to, am important" is the attitude which mires learning.

The only claim science has on anyone's attention or interest is the ability of a science to make phenomena workable and align that phenomena for better understanding. A body of data which does not accomplish this is not only not a science, it is a pretense and a humbuggery.[1] Thus, if you are working with any idea that the human mind is "too complex to understand," you are taking the stand of those who failed. The problem of resolving the human mind was enormously difficult. The solution of the operation and difficulties of the human mind is very simple.

1. **humbuggery:** pretense; sham.

We have three levels of operation. They are *thought, emotion* and *effort*. Thought produces motion or action through the medium of emotion. Motion and effort in general produce thought directly but also through the medium of emotion.

Thought is without time. It is instantaneous. Emotion, where its band rests in thought, is also without time. Effort and action contain time. A motion is a change of position in space. A change of position requires time. The common partner of time and space is motion. To have motion we have to have space and time. To have *emotion* we do not need time. And there is no time whatever in thought. This is the theoretical background. It doesn't much matter whether it is clearly understood or not.

An individual is a collection of "memories" going back to his first appearance on Earth. In other words, he is the composite of all his facsimiles plus his impulse *to be*. Individuality depends upon facsimiles. The very character and shape of the body, its genetic blueprint which says whether one has one head or two, is a composite of facsimiles, according to theory and evidences.

The facsimiles which occasion behavior were initially counter-efforts. All facsimiles contain counter-efforts. The body and personality are actually old counter-efforts which "I" has turned into efforts. Thoughts are timeless. You can close your eyes and see, in thought, some item which you well know is since vanished in the MEST universe. You have it as a facsimile still. You can, in thought, go back and be a small child. You cannot go back in body and change the past. That you can go back in thought tells us that the thought must be right here in present time too. In other words, you as mind can handle yesterday as thought. Thought is timeless. Thoughts are filed by your concept of when they happened. As long as you know the time tab of any thought, it is yours completely. When you do not know the time tab of a thought, you no longer control it.

People are very fond of saying they have "bad memories." They use this as a social excuse and to avoid recalling failures. The memory by these processes repairs rapidly until a person can recall things at will. His ability to recall things depends upon his ability to read the time tabs on his facsimiles, so to speak. In other words, so long as he recalls accurately, he is in control of the facsimile. When he cannot recall accurately, he is not in control of the facsimile.

At the Foundation we repair psychotics, the despair of thousands of years of civilized man, in a relatively short period of time. For two thousand years they have been giving psychotics shocks, restraints and operations—there has been no change. Freud alone suggested a change but he didn't have the reason why nor the effectiveness, and today, in major institutions, these antique methods pass for "modern" treatment. Out of our present body of knowledge we are restoring the sanity and effectiveness of psychotics, a thing which has never before been done with regularity or a guarantee of success. We even restore psychotics who have been given "modern" treatments, shock and the rest of it. How is this done?

Handle it this way: an insane person cannot reason or control himself. That means he cannot handle his facsimiles. By a series of precise steps the auditor gives the psychotic back the control of the facsimiles. These steps are as follows:

1. By mimicry (a form of communication), tactile (the most direct communication) and by general ARC we get the psychotic into communication with one human being, the auditor. This is sometimes long and difficult and is the most arduous step. It can be assisted by giving the psychotic MEST—time and space and removing restraints.

2. The auditor then works to get the psychotic into contact with present time. He calls attention to objects and the general environment until the psychotic sees that these are real. When the auditor knows the psychotic knows the reality of beds and walls, he turns attention to the psychotic himself as a being. He establishes the fact with the psychotic that the psychotic controls his own hands and feet and body.

3. At this stage the auditor may introduce the psychotic into association with other people and a wider environment. This is again more present time. The auditor *never* evaluates anything for the psychotic. The psychotic is insane because of too much evaluation by others and will slump if somebody starts thinking for him again.

4. The next step is to get the psychotic to evaluate something. This may be as mild as whether or not hamburgers are good to eat. The psychotic decides on an evaluation. Then many evaluations in present time.

5. Now the psychotic is asked to make minor decisions in present time plus action on those decisions. This includes getting him to decide to accept something and to decide to throw something away, for the handling of MEST is not unlike the handling of thoughts, and to a psychotic, thoughts are as solid as MEST.

6. The next step is to get the psychotic to recall something, no matter how general, about his past. He is asked to recall things until he strikes an incident he *really knows is real*. It is real to him. It is a real memory. This is another up point in his tone, as each of these steps listed are. But it is the big point. He has recognized as

real one of his own facsimiles. He isn't coaxed into admitting it is real. He recalls and knows that it really happened. He is then made to recall many such incidents. *He is never invalidated or argued with about what he thinks is real. The auditor simply ignores the hallucinations and accepts a real memory at last.*

7. The succeeding step is to get the psychotic to recall a past evaluation, a time when he made up his mind about the character or quality of something. The specific moment of evaluation is attained. Then the psychotic is made to recall a decision he has made in the past. Many evaluations and decisions are thus recalled.

8. The psychotic is now questioned about the times he has helped people. If possible, heavy failures are avoided. When he has recalled times when he has helped people and knows each incident recalled is real and actually happened, one goes to the next step.

9. The auditor now tries to locate the decision, the exact instant, with all perceptions possible, when the psychotic decided to go crazy. There may be many such decisions. These are recalled many times each.

10. The psychotic is now questioned on the subject of departed or failed relatives or friends until one is discovered who went mad. This is the location of a goal continuation for another.

11. Now the psychotic is worked on the subject of sympathy, what he has had to do to get sympathy, what sympathy he has given others. Probably a grief charge will come into view and can be run.

The individual about step 8 is no longer classifiable as very psychotic, by step 10 he is at worst neurotic. And he can be processed by counter-emotion, regret and other techniques.

This is outlined to give you some sort of an idea of what psychosis is and how sanity is restored. It is the condition of being unable to handle one's facsimiles. Sanity is restored by restoring an individual's ability, little by little, to handle his facsimiles.

But by what mechanism does an individual become unable to handle his memories? There are several answers but the main one is counter-emotion.

Counter-emotion is felt as the "atmosphere" around a person or place. Ask anyone to recall the "feel" of the "atmosphere" of an area or a person and he can reexperience it at least in part.

Emotion, according to present theory, can be laid down by anyone against anyone. The emotions of A can be infiltrated into the facsimiles of B. The thoughts of A, similarly, can be infiltrated into the thoughts of B, but so far as we are concerned at this writing, the mechanisms of thought and counter-thought are not well known. Emotion and counter-emotion are easily established.

How does one human being control another? High on the Tone Scale it is by letting the individual control himself as thoroughly as possible. Below 2.0, in the misemotion band, a human being seeks to control or destroy another by counter-emotion and counter-thought.

The atmosphere surrounding a misemotion person is easily sensed. When one advances a facsimile to a misemotion person, misemotion is immediately thrown into that facsimile. Effort is transferred by physical contact. Emotion is simply transferred by anger, fear, argument, sympathy, etc., from a misemotional person into the facsimiles of another. You may have noticed how you can become less sure of yourself or uneasy around people who are embarrassed or uneasy or afraid. This is a control mechanism. You are getting your facsimiles "colored" by a foreign emotion.

Every facsimile you advance, with argument or persuasion, toward a misemotional person gets counter-emotion thrown into it. *That counter-emotion takes your facsimile out of your own control and puts it into the control of the misemotional person.*

Nothing is easier to prove. You have noticed probably, in Lock Scanning, that certain persons were "occluded" or that the whole track was occluded. That occluded person was misemotional. The facsimiles you displayed around that person have their emotion on them, not yours. Your thought, then, has ceased to control such facsimiles. They do not come to view when called for by you. They are "occluded." The facsimiles aren't owned by you any longer but by the misemotional person.

One by one your facsimiles can be taken out of your control by misemotional persons. The end result is no further ownership of your own facsimiles or you. The end result is control by the environment, not self-control, misemotion instead of self-confidence. Doubt and fear of acting. In short, reactions such as those which appear along the lower band of the big chart. Slowed reaction time and illnesses and chronic pains result from these facsimiles which are no longer under your control. Misemotion has swamped them, occluded them, and so they can hurt you.

There is another, even simpler subject in counter-thought. You think one thing, somebody else thinks another. Their thought is counter to your thought. Live a while around somebody low on the scale and your thoughts get swamped by counter-thought. This is rehabilitated simply by running the ideas of another and the moment they expressed them.

Counter-emotion and counter-thought can become sufficiently serious so as to give you the illusion of having the facsimiles of another. This is a last extreme. This is hallucination.

Take a person who is normally occluded in your memory. Think back to a time when this person told you a story or an incident. You may have no view of that person telling the story, but instead a view of the activity in the story. This is a dub-in occasioned by their misemotion. The end product of this is to have the time track of some misemotional person with fake perceptions upon it. This is hallucination complete.

A misemotional person can become occluded not only in recall but also in present time. Such a person blurs out. When they come into the room, one has the illusion of the light failing slightly.

We all have the ambition to see a bright world. The thing which makes it unbright, in the main, is the misemotion we carry on our facsimiles from the atmospheres of misemotion in which we have dwelt.

Here is an exercise:

Go to a place on the track where there is an occlusion. Now try to feel the misemotion which might be in the atmosphere. Experience this counter-emotion by running through the incident swiftly many times.

A pain might have turned on. If so, continue to run this counter-emotion until the pain is gone. You probably are not running the full length of the incident.

New data appeared to you from that occluded area. Your own thoughts and feelings in that area began to brighten. You knew what you were thinking about and saying after you had run it a few times. This exercise is the one necessary to restore recall perception on occluded people and areas.

Another exercise:

Go to a place in recall where a normally occluded person is telling you a story or an incident. Find an area where you are getting the picture of the story, not the picture of the person telling it. Run the counter-emotion of the picture several times until you get a view of the person telling you the incident.

This is how people get occluded. A misemotional person specializes in telling people what to think and what the people think. Occlusion of childhood and hallucinatory pictures of childhood are occasioned by telling the child what happened to him, often and in detail. This knocks out the facsimiles of the child and substitutes either occlusion or a false picture.

Run the misemotion or any counter-emotion of times when you were told what had happened to you. Run these until the occlusion vanishes or the picture goes away. Don't necessarily go back to the incident being talked about.

List five people who are occluded on your track.

1.

2.

3.

4.

5.

Run the atmosphere around these occlusions until each one appears in view. If pictures of what they say turn up, run the pictures until the person turns up instead.

Warning: You will hit sympathy and a "desire" for sympathy from every one of these persons. Don't stop lock-scanning in a burst of contrition and fly to or write these people if they are still alive. Your mind will change about them.

List five people in your life who had different ideas about things than yourself.

1.

2.

3.

4.

5.

Now lock-scan through all incidents or counter-ideas for each person listed. Pick up their thought and then your thought in each incident.

List the names or locations of all the schools you attended.

1.

2.

3.

4.

5.

Now lock-scan the atmosphere of every classroom and teacher of each school in turn as counter-emotion.

Now lock-scan the pupils, friends and enemies, of each school in turn as counter-emotion.

Now lock-scan the teachers and schools as counter-thought to your thought, each one in turn.

Now lock-scan the pupils, enemies and friends, as counter-thought to your thought, each one in turn.

List five persons whom you consider to have wronged you.

1.

2.

3.

4.

5.

Lock-scan each time you saw each, with attention to counter-emotion.

Lock-scan each time you communicated to or saw each, with attention to counter-thought.

Let us now consider another phenomenon about emotion. This is the *emotional curve*.

On the Tone Scale you will find a difference of height between various emotions and misemotions. The emotional curve is the drop or rise from one level of emotion to another.

Can you find a time when you were happy and suddenly became sad?

This is easy. Experience or get a concept of how you would feel if you were happy and then how you would feel if you became sad. Then experience the change from happiness to sadness. Now find a situation where you were happy and became sad. Run this curve.

Who was present? Run the drop in tone as your own emotion. Then run the drop in tone as counter-emotion, the atmosphere change.

Run the emotional curve from happiness to sadness several times until you have full recovery on your own ideas and counter-thought. What did you think? What did the other say?

There are two emotional curves. One is the emotional curve you experience directly in yourself. The other is the counter-emotional curve, where you feel a change in tone in the atmosphere.

This is an auditor tool and is used to locate the *service facsimile* of the preclear.

17

The Tenth Act

17

The Tenth Act

For the auditor, if you are being audited part time or full time, the Tenth Act is the running out, by *thought*, *effort* and *emotion*, of the *service facsimile*. He will discover it from the data you have already written in this book, by looking you over for malfunction and by running emotional curves until you run into the front end of the incident.

An individual with a very thorough knowledge from additional texts on this science might be able to run the service facsimile itself. But several things militate against it, the first of them being that the preclear will try to run it out of valence (as somebody else); the second, that he considers it valuable and so doesn't want to lose it, and the third being that it takes a preclear so very much longer to run his own service facsimile than it takes an auditor.

18

The Eleventh Act

18

The Eleventh Act

This entire Act is addressed to the subject of *sympathy.*

Probably you could kill a man with sympathy. It has been done.

There are three levels of healing: the first is to do something efficient about the condition; the next, if the first can't be done, is to make the patient comfortable; the third, if he can't be made comfortable, is to give him sympathy. That is in accordance with old medical practice. However, sympathy is a terrible thing but is considered to be a very valuable thing.

The survival value of sympathy is this: When an individual is hurt or immobilized, he cannot fend for himself, get himself food, defend himself. If he is to survive he must count upon another or others to care for him. His bid for such care is the enlistment of the sympathy of others. This is practical. The cheerful good fellowship of the weak, crippled or ill is part of this mechanism. If men weren't sympathetic, none of us would be alive.

The nonsurvival value of sympathy is this: An individual fails in some activity or effort to help. He then considers himself incapable of surviving by himself. Even though he isn't sick actually, he makes a bid for sympathy.

When a person, not acutely ill or immobilized by injury, is making a bid for sympathy, he considers that he has failed so badly that he cannot by himself continue on in life. His self-confidence is undermined. He is not able to handle himself well. Counter-emotion and counter-thought have garbled his facsimiles. He feels he has to have sympathy to get along. And he displays an illness or disability, to gain sympathy. This is mechanical and is not to be disparaged: The person is actually in need of help. And almost every human being is prone to this error. Almost everyone will make a bid for sympathy by holding out some old facsimile. A psychosomatic illness is at once an explanation of failure and a bid for sympathy. That does not make the sympathy, when received, less sweet. And it does not make the ill any less painful.

One is peculiarly liable to sympathy bids around his parents and family. The worst case an auditor can encounter is one which wants auditing only for the auditor's sympathy and wants to retain the service facsimile because it is a sympathy source. The answer to this is to get the preclear far enough up the Tone Scale so that he is sufficiently self-confident not to need any sympathy. Only then, in some cases, will the service facsimile (the technical term for the facsimile the preclear uses to gain sympathy) surrender to auditing.

The purpose of this Act is to pick up sympathy facsimiles.

In other works on this science you will find in detail the role of self-determinism. We are all self-determined, natively. *Nothing* which we do is beyond self-determined action.

When you make a decision, it is *made*.

A later part of this processing deals thoroughly with this.

Nobody ever became ill without wanting to be ill at some earlier moment in his life. Here is a polio case, in bed two years. She became ill because she felt sorry for another little girl who got polio and so decided to get it herself. It was a clear-cut decision, followed by two long years in bed.

If you doubt that you ever wished to be ill, what about school? Didn't you ever beg off by a plaint[1] of being sick? How many times have you done this?

Scan through each and every time you decided to get sick.

Scan through all the reasons you decided to be ill.

When you have completed this exercise until you have extroverted on the subject, begin on the following:

Locate a moment when you felt sympathy for something. Scan through this moment over and over until it is desensitized.

Scan now the counter-emotion to your sympathy in that same incident.

Scan the sympathetic thought in that incident.

Scan the counter-thought in that incident, if any.

These four steps are a pattern for single incidents. After you have scanned just so many of these incidents you will find that sympathy, all up and down the track, seems to be resolving.

---

1. **plaint:** a complaint.

On the same subject, take up the following people.

Scan every incident you can find containing sympathy by you for them on the above pattern. (Omit any you did not have.)

Mother. Father. Guardian. Father's grandmother. Father's mother. Father's grandfather. Father's father. Mother's grandmother. Mother's mother. Mother's grandfather. Mother's father. Aunts. Great-aunts. Uncles. Great-uncles. Playmates. Marital partners. Teachers. Dogs. Cats. Horses. Goldfish. Children. Dolls. Toys. Animals. Birds. Possessions. Scenes. Houses. Beds.

Scan now the following story characters for sympathy or other emotion (omit any you were not acquainted with but be sure you didn't know them): Tiny Tim.[2] Little Orphan Annie.[3] Any Eugene Field[4] poem. Angels. Little Nell.[5] Any other story character.

Now we will reverse the process:

Scan any sympathy given you by any of the list of relatives and people above. Scan each incident in detail. The incident may include sickness; if so, scan it until any symptoms you pick up vanish again.

(By scanning emotion and counter-emotion, facsimiles drop off.)

---

2. **Tiny Tim:** character from the novel *A Christmas Carol* by Charles Dickens (1812–70, English).

3. **Little Orphan Annie:** character in a comic strip of the same name.

4. **Field, Eugene:** (1850–95) American poet and journalist, best known as poet of children's verse.

5. **Little Nell:** character in the novel *The Old Curiosity Shop* by Charles Dickens (1812–70, English).

Scan selectively, on sympathy and counter-emotion, the following: Yourself. For your eyes. For your mouth. For your ears. For your head. For your arms. For your hands. For your internal organs. For your stomach. For your legs. For your feet. For your back. For the genitals. For your life.

Scan sympathy and counter-emotion for each of the following: Every group. Every state or nation. Every population. For man in general. For the world.

Scan sympathy and counter-emotion for each of the following: Trees. Christmas trees. Any life form. The Supreme Being.

Now review all this analytically. You will discover the following: Before you felt sympathy, you offended in some way. You did something. Then you were sorry for it. This offense may have taken place years before your sympathy came about or only minutes. This is the emotional curve of sympathy. It goes from antagonism or anger down to sympathy.

You know now where and on what dynamic you felt the greatest sympathy. Was it for Mother? All right, let's find out where we first offended Mother, hurt her in fact.

Scan every subject of sympathy early enough to find where you offended. Scan out the offense. If it doesn't come clear, scan regret as an emotion until it does come clear. If you encounter a grief charge, run it as a straight incident, as contained in an earlier Act.

List now the chief objects of sympathy.

Check each one again and scan it again.

This used to be called a "guilt complex." This process undoes them.

19

The Twelfth Act

19

The Twelfth Act

It is time that we took another glance at "buttons." There are several things in particular that each human being finds aberrative and has in common.

By Lock Scanning, run each one of the following with attention to counter-emotion and counter-thought:

Hiding things. Hiding things from self. Hiding things from parents. Hiding things from employers. Hiding things from teachers. Hiding things from the public.

Talking. The feeling that people will talk. The fear that you may talk. The secrets you dare not tell. The secrets you promised not to tell. Being talked to. Fear of talking to somebody. Fear of talking to crowds. Talking behind people's backs. Methods of avoiding being talked to. Being talked into things.

Enduring. Enduring conversation. Enduring situations. Waiting. (Avoid physical-pain incidents.)

Keeping things. Keeping pets. Keeping toys. Keeping possessions. Your decisions to keep things. Your failure to keep things. Keeping people.

Losing things. Losing pets. Losing possessions. Losing people. Being left. (As a common, not a final, occurrence.)

Taking things seriously. Taking tasks seriously. Taking people seriously. Regarding situations as serious. Regarding work as serious. Why you regarded these things seriously. Moments when you decided to take things seriously.

Not taking things seriously. Efforts not to take things seriously. Efforts to get others not to take things seriously. Being told to take things seriously. Refusing to take things seriously. Regret at not taking something seriously.

Trying to stop things. Stopping people. Stopping situations. Stopping mechanical things. (You may find you have tried to stop time often. That's when you get a fixed visio. Simply run off the regret.)

Starting things. Starting people. Starting situations. Starting mechanical things. Starting children.

Changing things. Decisions not to change things. Decisions to change self. Decisions to change others. Efforts to change others. Changing directions of things.

Moving things. Moving people. Moving heavy objects. Moving yourself. Resisting being moved out of bed your entire lifetime.

Owning things. Efforts to own things. Efforts to keep others from controlling what you own. Efforts not to own things.

Care of clothing. Times you couldn't select clothing. Times you were forced to care for clothing. Times when you couldn't wear clothing you owned. Times when you couldn't have clothing.

Care of person. Times when you were forced to care for person. Times when somebody else forced care on you. Times when you decided not to take care of yourself.

To be: Times when you decided to be something. Times when you decided you couldn't be something. Times when you decided to change being what you were.

Not to be: Times when you decided to quit. Decisions to stop being what you were.

Habits: Times when you first decided to have any habit you have. Times when you decided not to have the habits. Times when you decided to have the habits you have.

Knowing: Times when you decided you knew.

Not knowing: Times when you decided you did not know.

Doubts: Times when you doubted yourself. Times when you doubted others. Decisions that you could not trust. Decisions that you could trust.

Wrong: Times when you decided you had been wrong. Times when you were afraid you were wrong. Times when another said you were wrong. Times when evidence turned up that you had been wrong.

Right: Times when you hoped you weren't right. Times when you found you were right. Fear that you would not be right.

Time: Incidents where you decided you didn't have any time. Times when you said you didn't have time. Times when somebody else didn't have time. Times when you tried to get out of something by saying you didn't have time. Times when you felt it was too late to start but that it should have been done.

The past: Times when you decided to put all the past behind you. Times when you decided the past was too terrible.

The present: Your decisions about the present, good or bad.

The future: Times when you decided the future was doubtful. Times when you wanted the future to be like the past. Times when you were afraid of the future. Times when you feared dying. Times when you wanted to die. Times when you were glad to have a bright future. Times when your plans for the future had to be violently changed. Times when somebody else planned your future. Times when you planned another's future. Hopelessness about the future. Hope for the future. The hopelessness of another about the future. The hopes of another for the future. Failure to measure up to what another hoped for your future.

Agreement: Times when you were forced to agree but didn't want to. Times when you forced others to agree. Times when you were prevented from agreeing. Times when you prevented others from agreeing. Times when you were glad to agree.

Communication: Times when you were forced to communicate. Times when you were prevented from communicating. Times when you forced others to communicate. Times when you prevented others from communicating. Times when you wanted to communicate.

Affinity: Times when you were forced to like somebody. Times when you were prevented from liking somebody. Times when you forced another to like you. Times when you prevented another from liking you. Times when you decided you liked somebody.

Individuality: Times when you felt you weren't yourself. Times when you decided not to be yourself. Times when you were forced to be yourself. Times when you were inhibited from being yourself. Times when you tried to change another person. Times when you decided not to change somebody else.

Truth: Times when you decided to lie. The reasons why you decided to lie. Times when you felt better lying. Times when lying got you into trouble. Times when you decided never to lie again.

Faith: Times when you decided to have faith in the Supreme Being. Times when you decided not to have faith in the Supreme Being. Times when you decided not to have faith in your government. Times when you decided to have faith in your government. Times when you decided to have faith in yourself. Times when you didn't have faith in yourself. Times when another did not have any faith in you.

Anger: All the times you have been angry, with attention to your emotion and counter-emotion and the reasons you were angry.

Fear: All the times you have been afraid, with attention to your emotion and the atmosphere in which you were and reasons why you were afraid. Scan the first times you decided to be afraid.

Cowardice: Scan all the times you considered yourself a coward. Scan the times you considered others cowardly.

Embarrassment: Scan all the times you have been embarrassed. Scan the times you have been embarrassed for others.

Shame: Scan all the times you have been ashamed. Scan the times you have been ashamed for others.

Grief: Spot and run every grief charge on your case. List them in the blank below, then run them. Run counter-emotion and regret until charge comes into view. Then run it as a single incident.

Apathy: Scan every person around you who has ever been in apathy. Scan every time you yourself felt apathy. Scan the times when you sought to lift others out of apathy. Scan the times when others sought to lift you out of apathy.

Scan all the times when you have been supremely happy. Scan the times you have made others happy.

Run emotional curves on the times when you tried to enthuse others and failed.

Run the times you enthused others and succeeded.

20

The
Thirteenth Act

20

The Thirteenth Act

The subject of blame and regret is an interesting one. Blame of self and blame of others produce interesting results in recalls. Facsimiles can become clouded with blame and regret.

This is the subject of cause and effect.

An individual natively desires to be cause. He tries not to become a bad effect.

You try to help people and people try to help you because you and they want to be cause. When something bad happens, neither one wishes to be cause.

You want to be an effect. Then you find the effect bad. You try not to be an effect. And then you blame something or somebody.

Blaming yourself or others for being a cause is to deny yourself full control of your facsimiles. You say somebody caused something. You make them responsible. They are then cause. This is a powerful position. It ends up with your having given them control over a facsimile or many facsimiles. If you blame somebody hard enough and long enough, you have kept on electing them as cause until they are much more powerful than yourself.

If you blame your mother, for instance, you make your mother cause and must then obey her. And your facsimiles relating to her or to your whole life are out of your control. If you blame yourself, this is an admitted failure and again you have facsimiles out of control.

You blame somebody, you elect them as cause. This makes you an effect of their cause. As an effect you are thus placed well down the Tone Scale.

You desire to be an effect in some quarter and thereafter you may continue to be an effect and will go down the scale to a point where you may develop psychosomatic ills.

There are certain main spheres where one wishes to be an effect. Here we have the importance of aberration on the second dynamic, sex. You wish to have the pleasure of sex. This is yourself electing yourself as an effect. As an effect you can then be given pain on the second dynamic.

You wish to be pleasantly an effect in eating. You elect yourself an effect. You can thereafter be affected by pain in the food department. The basis of ulcers or any stomach trouble including constipation is the original desire to eat.

You wish to be amused and entertained. Thus amusement channels, sight, sound, rhythm, can become aberrated by pain.

It is a natural law that one cannot be aberrated without one's own consent. One must wish to be an effect before he can become an effect. If he becomes an effect then he can later become "effected" unpleasantly by counter-efforts.

If you want to be an effect of your marital or sexual partner, or any sexual act, you open the door to being an unpleasant effect.

Examine the column of the big chart between Cause and Effect. This is a gradient scale of causes and effects.

Freud was right in selecting sex as being very aberrative. Before him thousands of years of mystics knew they had to abstain from material or physical pleasures and sex in order to remain high and saintly. They did not know the mechanism at work. We now do. The moment they wanted to be an effect, they could become, in that channel, an unpleasant as well as a pleasant effect and so go down the Tone Scale.

There are several conditions relating to this. One is the desire not to be a cause. One is the desire not to be an effect. One is the desire to prevent something or somebody else from being a cause. One is the desire to prevent somebody or something else from being an effect.

In sex one may not desire to be the cause of children. This would be for either a man or a woman. Children, in this society, can be embarrassing or expensive. One desires at the same time to cause a sexual partner pleasure. Here is desire not to be a cause fighting with the desire to be a cause. The result is conflict, aberration, impotence, sex punishment and irregular practices.

In sex, again, one desires greatly to be an effect for the sake of pleasure. One wishes to experience the pleasure of sex. He does not want to experience the pain of childbirth for himself or his partner nor does he wish the effect of disease. Nor does he wish to be the effect of public antagonism toward sexual practice. Thus his desire for effect comes in conflict with his desire not to be effect and the result is aberration, impotence, glandular interruption, marital breakdowns, divorces, suicide and sudden death.

In food, cause and effect work similarly to sex. One wishes to be pleasantly affected by the flavor of substance of food. He may not want to have the effect of the work he has to do to eat or the propitiation he has to give to eat. He wants to be cause. He is running a carbon-oxygen engine which has to have the effect of food. People low on the Tone Scale use this sure route to making a person into an effect by denying food or forcing people to eat food. The society uses this effect to get work done.

Low-scale mothers are very strict with their children about food. This is a sure method of control. By forcing the child to be a non-self-determined effect about food, the mother can control the child in many other ways. All low-scale control is done by forcing the individual to be an effect where the individual naturally has to be an effect. Where a naturally desired effect can be enforced by command, the enforcer can gain a wide control simply by continual demonstration that the target individual is an effect, not a cause.

The sexual sphere is peculiarly liable to cause and effect action because of the communication. Tactile is the most direct method of sensory communication. It is much more effective than talk. A close communication with a low-scale person brings down as well the affinity and the reality levels. If a sexual partner is demanding or insatiable, that partner elects the other into being an unwilling cause and denies his right to the effect and thus makes ruin of a personality. An individual aberrated enough about sex will do strange things to be a cause or an effect. He will substitute punishment for sex. He will pervert others.

Homosexuality comes from this manifestation and from the

manifestation of life continuation for others. A boy whose mother is dominant will try to continue her life from any failure she has. A girl whose father is dominant will try to continue his life from any failure he has. The mother or the father were cause in the child's eyes. The child elected himself successor to cause. Break this life continuum concept by running sympathy and grief for the dominant parent and then run off the desires to be an effect and their failures, and the homosexual is rehabilitated. Homosexuality is about 1.1 on the Tone Scale. So is general promiscuity.

The facsimiles of an individual can become considerably scrambled by masturbation. Practically all the ape family and man masturbate. Masturbation is a prohibition result. It couldn't drive anyone crazy. But it can make the individual pull old sex facsimiles into present time for self-stimulation and opens the door for him to desire facsimiles to be in present time. After a while he will be pulling pain facsimiles into present time.

These are the exercises of Cause and Effect Processing:

Scan through every time you desired not to be a cause sexually.

Scan through every time you regretted being a sexual cause.

Scan through every time you desired not to be an effect sexually.

Scan through every time you regretted being an effect sexually.

Scan through every time you desired to be a sexual cause.

Scan through every time you desired to be a sexual effect.

(Don't forget that scanning is done until you are extroverted on the subject.)

Scan every time you called up an old sexual experience for your amusement.

Scan every time a sexual partner was demanding.

Scan every time a sexual partner refused sex.

Scan every failure concerning sex.

Scan every time you obeyed a sexual partner about anything.

Scan every time you resented somebody's sexual conversation.

Scan every time you enjoyed somebody's sexual conversation.

Scan every time you tried to hide something about sex.

Now let us repeat these operations on the subject of food:

Scan every time you desired food.

Scan every time you were forced to eat.

Scan every time you worried about food.

Scan every time you blamed food for an illness.

Scan every feeling of queasiness about food until any physical sensation is gone.

Now let us go into entertainment:

Scan every time you tried to entertain somebody and failed.

Scan every time you wanted to be entertained and weren't.

Scan every time somebody wanted to be entertained and you didn't want to.

Scan every time you were bored with entertainment.

Scan every time you wanted to retain the sensation of having been entertained.

Now let us go into perceptions in general:

Scan every time you did not want to be touched.

Scan every time you were forced to touch something.

Scan every time you wanted to touch something and couldn't.

Scan every time you touched a sexual partner.

Scan every time you didn't want to look.

Scan every time you wanted to be pleased by looking.

Scan every time you wished things looked as good as they used to.

Scan every regret you've ever had about sight.

Scan every time you decided you couldn't see well.

Scan every time you were told you couldn't see.

Scan every time you agreed you couldn't see.

Scan every time you didn't want to listen.

Scan every time you wanted to hear and couldn't.

Scan every time you wanted to hear something pleasant.

Scan every time your ears rang.

Scan every time you decided something was wrong with your hearing.

Scan every time you tasted something bad.

Scan every time you tasted something good.

Scan every time your mother pushed you away.

Scan every time you wanted a good effect in your stomach and failed.

Scan every time you looked with favor on a bottle. (Get way back early on this one.)

Scan every time you told somebody you were tired.

Scan every time you told somebody you didn't feel well.

Scan every time you felt sympathy for a blind man.

Scan every time you felt sympathy for a deaf man.

Scan every time you smelled something bad, and the counter-emotion.

Scan all the times you smelled something good.

Scan all the times you hid the fact that some effect pleased you.

Scan all the times you wanted to be cause.

Scan all the times you concluded you were important.

Scan all the times you concluded you were not important.

Scan all the times you concluded you were nobody.

Scan all the times you concluded you were somebody.

Scan all the times you thought you were not valuable.

Scan all the times you thought you were valuable.

Scan all the times you tried to convince somebody you were important.

Scan all the times you tried to convince somebody you were somebody.

Scan all the times you tried to convince somebody you were valuable.

Scan all the times you tried to stop sound during sex.

Scan all the times you stopped or interrupted sex.

Scan all the times you started sex and failed.

Scan all the times you wanted to hear sounds during sex.

Scan all the times you wanted sexual conversation to affect you.

Scan all the times you resented sexual conversation.

Scan all the times you resented "dirty jokes."

Scan off the counter-emotion of each exercise above, each in turn.

As you have read here before and as you have come to suspect in your processing, your own decisions and evaluations are the most important items in the entire process.

What you decide is *law* to you. What you evaluate is evaluation to you.

Self-confidence is nothing more than belief in one's ability to decide and in one's decisions.

Most people think they have unconscious minds or backgrounds of motivation simply because they have refused their own power to decide.

Negation of decision, refusal of decision, letting others decide, are the most powerful sources of aberration. They apply to any and all subjects.

This section is devoted to picking up each and every postulate you can now reach in your whole lifetime. A postulate is a decision you make to yourself or to others. You make one, then afterwards conditions change and you make a second one. This makes the first one wrong. You make a postulate as cause and then, by having lived through some instants of time, become an effect of your own cause.

A computer could not work if you kept leaving its totals on the calculator for the next problem. That is what you do with decisions. They have to be made. Sweep them up before making more. It is a new method of thinking and one that keeps you happy. No need to be afraid of making decisions. Simply sweep up old decisions. You make New Year's resolutions. And you make them into the teeth of old resolutions which were different. Then you don't keep your new resolutions and you tell yourself you are weak-willed. You aren't weak-willed, you are simply obeying yourself as of yesterday.

Emotion and effort cover up these postulates. They should be free and clear by now and indeed should blow at a glance. There are two parts to every postulate. There is the evaluation of data and the decision itself.

When you pick up an old decision, also pick up the reason you made it. They "blow" very quickly.

Scan through every decision, with its reason why, you have made about women.

Scan every decision about men.

Scan every decision about yourself.

Scan every decision about the world.

Scan every decision about dogs.

Scan every decision about cats.

Scan every decision about horses.

Scan every decision about fish.

Scan every decision about food.

Scan every decision about sex.

Scan every decision about clothing.

Scan every decision about shoes.

Scan every decision about houses.

Scan every decision about cars.

Scan every decision about scenery.

Scan every decision about criminals.

Scan every decision about newspapers.

Scan every decision about your mother.

Scan every decision about your father.

Scan every decision about philosophy.

Scan every decision about psychology.

Scan every decision about education.

Scan every decision about money.

Scan every decision about work.

Scan every decision about life.

Scan every decision about God.

Scan every decision about fighting.

Scan every decision about sin.

Scan every decision about obeying.

Scan every decision about making others obey.

Scan every decision about government.

Scan every decision to apologize.

Scan every decision to be jealous.

Scan every decision to be angry.

Scan every decision to help.

Scan every conclusion that you have failed.

Scan every decision that you have succeeded.

Scan every decision that you are a good sexual partner.

Scan every decision that you are a poor sexual partner.

Scan every decision that any other is a good sexual partner.

Scan every decision that any other is a bad sexual partner.

Scan every decision to regret something.

Scan every decision to enjoy something.

Scan every time a contribution has been rejected.

Scan every time a contribution has been accepted.

Scan every decision to resent criticism.

Scan every decision to work for praise.

Scan every decision to quit.

Scan every decision to start.

Scan every decision to stop.

Scan every decision to change.

Scan every decision to wait.

Scan every decision to move.

Scan every conclusion that you are ill.

Scan every conclusion that you are well.

Scan every decision to resent something.

Scan every decision to be human.

21

The
Fourteenth Act

21

The Fourteenth Act

First review the earlier data about control centers. Then do the following:

Write down every time you considered yourself to have had a major failure.

Run each single incident consecutively from the moment you planned the action through the moment you realized you had failed through the possible resulting illness and to the moment when you felt cheerful again. Go through each incident in complete detail with counter-thought, counter-emotion and blame and regret, with all available perceptics, until the entire incident is in tone 4.0. That tone is laughter. Do not quit in boredom; that's only part way there.

Scan off all locks from each failure.

Now the next step:

Run every death of everyone you have known in this lifetime. Run regret and blame of self or others until the death shows up in complete detail. Run the death completely out. If you have difficulty, run every time you offended the dead person, every time you felt sympathy for the dead person, until the incident is in full view. Then run it completely. Remember to find and run any decision to try to make this person live or any regret that you didn't make this person live.

Run off the death of every pet similarly to people.

This should rehabilitate all control centers for this lifetime.

22

The Fifteenth Act

22

The Fifteenth Act

This is a review Act and is very necessary to a completion of processing.

Turn back to the beginning of the book and read all the text up to the processing section. That text will mean a great deal more to you now than it did before.

Now take the Second Act and review everything you did in it. There will be much more data for it and much more understanding.

Take each Act consecutively and do the complete Act again. Read the texts for the Acts and repeat all the exercises. New data will be found all up and down the line.

23

Definitions, Logics and Axioms

Definitions,
Logics and Axioms

These are the definitions, logics and axioms of this science. It should be borne in mind that these actually form epistemology, the science of knowledge. These cannot but embrace various fields and sciences. They are listed in this volume without further elucidation but will be found to be self-explanatory for the most part. Adequate phenomena exist to demonstrate the self-evidence of these definitions, postulates, logics and axioms.

The first section, the Logics, is separate from the Axioms only in that from the system of thinking so evaluated, the Axioms themselves flow. The word *logics* is used here to mean postulates pertaining to the organizational structure of alignment.

The Logics

Logic 1:   *Knowledge is a whole group or subdivision of a group of data or speculations or conclusions on data or methods of gaining data.*

Logic 2:   *A body of knowledge is a body of data, aligned or unaligned, or methods of gaining data.*

Logic 3:   *Any knowledge which can be sensed, measured or experienced by any entity is capable of influencing that entity.*
COROLLARY:[1] That knowledge which cannot be sensed, measured or experienced by any entity or type of entity cannot influence that entity or type of entity.

Logic 4:   *A datum is a symbol of matter, energy, space or time, or any combination thereof, in any universe, or the matter, energy, space or time itself, or any combination thereof, in any universe.*

---

1. **corollary:** a proposition that is incidentally proved in proving another proposition.

the more it is wrong from the viewpoint of the intended survivor.

COROLLARY: Any datum has only relative truth.

COROLLARY: Truth is relative to environments, experience and truth.

Logic 8:   *A datum can be evaluated only by a datum of comparable magnitude.*

Logic 9:   *A datum is as valuable as it has been evaluated.*

Logic 10:   *The value of a datum is established by the amount of alignment (relationship) it imparts to other data.*

Logic 11:   *The value of a datum or field of data can be established by its degree of assistance in survival or its inhibition to survival.*

Logic 12:   *The value of a datum or a field of data is modified by the viewpoint of the observer.*

Logic 13:   *Problems are resolved by compartmenting them into areas of similar magnitude and data, comparing them to data already known or partially known, and resolving each area. Data which cannot be known immediately may be resolved by addressing what is known and using its solution to resolve the remainder.*

Logic 14:   *Factors introduced into a problem or solution which do not derive from natural law but only from authoritarian command aberrate that problem or solution.*

Logic 15:   *The introduction of an arbitrary into a problem or solution invites the further introduction of arbitraries into problems and solutions.*

Logic 16:   *An abstract postulate must be compared to the universe to which it applies and brought into the category of things which can be sensed, measured or experienced in that universe before such postulate can be considered workable.*

Logic 17:   *Those fields which most depend upon authoritative opinion for their data least contain known natural law.*

Logic 18:   *A postulate is as valuable as it is workable.*

Logic 19:   *The workability of a postulate is established by the degree to which it explains existing phenomena already known, by the degree that it predicts new phenomena which when looked for will be found to exist, and by the degree that it does not require that phenomena which do not exist in fact be called into existence for its explanation.*

Logic 20:   *A science may be considered to be a large body of aligned data which has similarity in application and which has been deduced or induced from basic postulates.*

Logic 21:   *Mathematics are methods of postulating or resolving real or abstract data in any universe and integrating by symbolization of data, postulates and resolutions.*

Logic 22:   *The human mind* is an observer, postulator, creator and storage place of knowledge.*
   *The human mind by definition includes the awareness unit of the living organism, the observer, the computer of data, the spirit, the memory storage, the life force and the individual motivator of the living organism. It is used as distinct from the brain which can be considered to be motivated by the mind.

Logic 23:   *The human mind is a servomechanism[2] to any mathematics evolved or employed by the human mind.*

POSTULATE: The human mind and inventions of the human mind are capable of resolving any and all problems which can be sensed, measured or experienced directly or indirectly.

COROLLARY: The human mind is capable of resolving the problem of the human mind.

The borderline of solution of this science lies between *why* life is surviving and *how* life is surviving. It is possible to resolve *how* life is surviving without resolving *why* life is surviving.

Logic 24:   *The resolution of the philosophical, scientific and human studies (such as economics, politics, sociology, medicine, criminology, etc.) depends primarily upon the resolution of the problems of the human mind.*

NOTE: The primary step in resolving the broad activities of man could be considered to be the resolving of the activities of the mind itself. Hence, the Logics carry to this point and then proceed as axioms concerning the human mind, such axioms being substantiated as relative truths by much newly discovered phenomena. The ensuing axioms, from Logic 24, apply no less to the various "ologies" than they do to deaberrating or improving the operation of the mind. It should not be thought that the following axioms are devoted to the construction of anything as limited as a therapy, which is only incidental to the resolution of human aberration and such things as psychosomatic illnesses. These axioms are capable of such solution, as has been demonstrated, but such a narrow application would indicate a very narrow scope of view.

---

2. **servomechanism:** an electronic control system in which a hydraulic, pneumatic or other type of controlling mechanism is actuated and controlled by a low-energy signal.

The Axioms
of Dianetics

Axiom 1: The source of life is a static of peculiar and particular properties.

Axiom 2: At least a portion of the static called life is impinged upon the physical universe.

Axiom 3: That portion of the static of life which is impinged upon the physical universe has for its dynamic goal, survival and only survival.

Axiom 4: The physical universe is reducible to motion of energy operating in space through time.

Axiom 5: That portion of the static of life concerned with the life organisms of the physical universe is concerned wholly with motion.

Axiom 6: The life static has as one of its properties the ability to mobilize and animate matter into living organisms.

Axiom 7: The life static is engaged in a conquest of the physical universe.

Axiom 8:   The life static conquers the material universe by learning and applying the physical laws of the physical
universe.
SYMBOL: The symbol for the LIFE STATIC in use hereafter is the Greek letter THETA.

Axiom 9:   A fundamental operation of THETA in surviving is
bringing order into the chaos of the physical universe.

Axiom 10:   THETA brings order into chaos by conquering whatever
in MEST may be prosurvival and destroying whatever in
MEST may be contrasurvival, at least through the me-
dium of life organisms.
SYMBOL: The symbol for the PHYSICAL UNIVERSE in use
hereafter is MEST, from the first letters of the words
MATTER, ENERGY, SPACE and TIME, or the Greek letter
PHI.

Axiom 11:   A life organism is composed of matter and energy in
space and time, animated by THETA.
SYMBOL: Living organism or organisms will hereafter
be represented by the Greek letter LAMBDA.

Axiom 12:   The MEST part of the organism follows the laws of the
physical sciences. All LAMBDA is concerned with motion.

Axiom 13:   THETA operating through LAMBDA converts the forces of
the physical universe into forces to conquer the physical
universe.

Axiom 14:   THETA working upon physical universe motion must
maintain a harmonious rate of motion.
The limits of LAMBDA are narrow, both as to ther-
mal and mechanical motion.

Axiom 15:   LAMBDA *is the intermediate step in the conquest of the physical universe.*

Axiom 16:   *The basic food of any organism consists of light and chemicals.*
Organisms can exist only as higher levels of complexities because lower levels of converters exist.
THETA evolves organisms from lower to higher forms and supports them by the existence of lower converter forms.

Axiom 17:   THETA, *via* LAMBDA, *effects an evolution of* MEST.
In this we have the waste products of organisms on the one hand as those very complex chemicals which bacteria make and, on the other hand, we have the physical face of the Earth being changed by animals and men, such changes as grass holding mountains from eroding or roots causing boulders to break, buildings being built, and rivers being dammed. There is obviously an evolution in MEST in progress under the incursion of THETA.

Axiom 18:   LAMBDA, *even within a species, varies in its endowment of* THETA.

Axiom 19:   *The effort of* LAMBDA *is toward survival.*
The goal of LAMBDA *is survival.*
The penalty of failure to advance toward that goal is to succumb.
DEFINITION: Persistence is the ability to exert continuance of effort toward survival goals.

Axiom 20:   LAMBDA *creates, conserves, maintains, requires, destroys, changes, occupies, groups and disperses* MEST.
LAMBDA *survives by animating and mobilizing or destroying matter and energy in space and time.*

Axiom 21: LAMBDA *is dependent upon optimum motion. Motion which is too swift and motion which is too slow are equally contrasurvival.*

Axiom 22: THETA *and thought are similar orders of static.*

Axiom 23: *All thought is concerned with motion.*

Axiom 24: *The establishment of an optimum motion is a basic goal of reason.*
DEFINITION: LAMBDA is a chemical heat engine existing in space and time motivated by the life static and directed by thought.

Axiom 25: *The basic purpose of reason is the calculation or estimation of effort.*

Axiom 26: *Thought is accomplished by* THETA FACSIMILES *of physical universe, entities or actions.*

Axiom 27: THETA *is satisfied only with harmonious action or optimum motion and rejects or destroys action or motion above or below its tolerance band.*

Axiom 28: *The mind is concerned wholly with the estimation of effort.*
DEFINITION: Mind is the THETA command post of any organism or organisms.

Axiom 29: *The basic errors of reason are failure to differentiate amongst matter, energy, space and time.*

Axiom 30: *Rightness is proper calculation of effort.*

Axiom 31: *Wrongness is always miscalculation of effort.*

Axiom 32:   THETA *can exert itself directly or extensionally.*
THETA can direct physical application of the organism to the environment or, through the mind, can first calculate the action or extend, as in language, ideas.

Axiom 33:   *Conclusions are directed toward the inhibition, maintenance or accelerations of efforts.*

Axiom 34:   *The common denominator of all life organisms is motion.*

Axiom 35:   *Effort of an organism to survive or succumb is physical motion of a life organism at a given moment in time through space.*
DEFINITION: Motion is any change in orientation in space.
DEFINITION: Force is random effort.
DEFINITION: Effort is directed force.

Axiom 36:   *An organism's effort can be to remain at rest or persist in a given motion.*
Static state has position in time, but an organism which is remaining positionally in a static state, if alive, is still continuing a highly complex pattern of motion, such as the heartbeat, digestion, etc.
The efforts of organisms to survive or succumb are assisted, compelled or opposed by the efforts of other organisms, matter, energy, space and time.
DEFINITION: Attention is a motion which must remain at an optimum effort.
Attention is aberrated by becoming unfixed and sweeping at random or becoming too fixed without sweeping.
Unknown threats to survival when sensed cause

attention to sweep without fixing.
Known threats to survival when sensed cause attention to fix.

Axiom 37: *The ultimate goal of* LAMBDA *is infinite survival.*

Axiom 38: *Death is abandonment by* THETA *of a life organism or race or species where these can no longer serve* THETA *in its goals of infinite survival.*

Axiom 39: *The reward of an organism engaging upon survival activity is pleasure.*

Axiom 40: *The penalty of an organism failing to engage upon survival activity, or engaging in nonsurvival activity, is pain.*

Axiom 41: *The cell and virus are the primary building blocks of life organisms.*

Axiom 42: *The virus and cell are matter and energy animated and motivated in space and time by* THETA.

Axiom 43: THETA *mobilizes the virus and cell in colonial aggregations to increase potential motion and accomplish effort.*

Axiom 44: *The goal of viruses and cells is survival in space through time.*

Axiom 45: *The total mission of higher organisms, viruses and cells is the same as that of the virus and cell.*

Axiom 46: *Colonial aggregations of viruses and cells can be imbued with more* THETA *than they inherently contained.*
Life energy joins any group, whether a group of

organisms or group of cells composing an organism.
Here we have personal entity, individuation, etc.

Axiom 47: *Effort can be accomplished by* LAMBDA *only through the coordination of its parts toward goals.*

Axiom 48: *An organism is equipped to be governed and controlled by a mind.*

Axiom 49: *The purpose of the mind is to pose and resolve problems relating to survival and to direct the effort of the organism according to these solutions.*

Axiom 50: *All problems are posed and resolved through estimations of effort.*

Axiom 51: *The mind can confuse position in space with position in time. (Counter-efforts producing action phrases.)*

Axiom 52: *An organism proceeding toward survival is directed by the mind of that organism in the accomplishment of survival effort.*

Axiom 53: *An organism proceeding toward succumb is directed by the mind of that organism in the accomplishment of death.*

Axiom 54: *Survival of an organism is accomplished by the overcoming of efforts opposing its survival. (Note: Corollary for other dynamics.)*
DEFINITION: Dynamic is the ability to translate solutions into action.

Axiom 55: *Survival effort for an organism includes the dynamic thrust by that organism for the survival of itself, its procreation, its group, its subspecies, its species, all life organisms, material universe, the life static and, possibly, a Supreme Being. (Note: List of dynamics.)*

Axiom 56: *The cycle of an organism, a group of organisms or a species is inception, growth, re-creation, decay and death.*

Axiom 57: *The effort of an organism is directed toward the control of the environment for all the dynamics.*

Axiom 58: *Control of an environment is accomplished by the support of prosurvival factors along any dynamic.*

Axiom 59: *Any type of higher organism is accomplished by the evolution of viruses and cells into forms capable of better efforts to control or live in an environment.*

Axiom 60: *The usefulness of an organism is determined by its ability to control the environment or to support organisms which control the environment.*

Axiom 61: *An organism is rejected by* THETA *to the degree that it fails in its goals.*

Axiom 62: *Higher organisms can exist only in the degree that they are supported by the lower organisms.*

Axiom 63: *The usefulness of an organism is determined by the alignment of its efforts toward survival.*

Axiom 64: *The mind perceives and stores all data of the environment and aligns or fails to align these according to the time they were perceived.*
DEFINITION: A conclusion is the *THETA FACSIMILES* of a

group of combined data.

DEFINITION: A datum is a THETA FACSIMILE of physical action.

Axiom 65: *The process of thought is the perception of the present and the comparison of it to the perceptions and conclusions of the past in order to direct action in the immediate or distant future.*

COROLLARY: The attempt of thought is to perceive realities of the past and present in order to predict or postulate realities of the future.

Axiom 66: *The process by which life effects its conquest of the material universe consists in the conversion of the potential effort of matter and energy in space and through time to effect with it the conversion of further matter and energy in space and through time.*

Axiom 67: THETA *contains its own* THETA UNIVERSE *effort which translates into* MEST *effort.*

Axiom 68: *The single arbitrary in any organism is time.*

Axiom 69: *Physical universe perceptions and efforts are received by an organism as force waves, convert by facsimile into* THETA *and are thus stored.*

DEFINITION: Randomity is the misalignment through the internal or external efforts by other forms of life or the material universe of the efforts of an organism, and is imposed on the physical organism by counter-efforts in the environment.

Axiom 70: *Any cycle of any life organism is from static to motion to static.*

Axiom 71: The cycle of randomity is from static, through optimum, through randomity sufficiently repetitious or similar to constitute another static.

Axiom 72: There are two subdivisions to randomity: data randomity and force randomity.

Axiom 73: The three degrees of randomity consist of minus randomity, optimum randomity and plus randomity.
DEFINITION: Randomity is a component factor and necessary part of motion, if motion is to continue.

Axiom 74: Optimum randomity is necessary to learning.

Axiom 75: The important factors in any area of randomity are effort and counter-effort. (Note: As distinguished from near perceptions of effort.)

Axiom 76: Randomity amongst organisms is vital to continuous survival of all organisms.

Axiom 77: THETA affects the organism, other organisms and the physical universe by translating THETA FACSIMILES into physical efforts or randomity of efforts.
DEFINITION: The degree of randomity is measured by the randomness of effort vectors within the organism, amongst organisms, amongst races or species of organisms or between organisms and the physical universe.

Axiom 78: Randomity becomes intense in indirect ratio to the time in which it takes place, modified by the total effort in the area.

Axiom 79: Initial randomity can be reinforced by randomities of greater or lesser magnitude.

Axiom 80:   Areas of randomity exist in chains of similarity plotted against time. This can be true of words and actions contained in randomities. Each may have its own chain plotted against time.

Axiom 81:   Sanity consists of optimum randomity.

Axiom 82:   Aberration exists to the degree that plus or minus randomity exists in the environment or past data of an organism, group or species, modified by the endowed self-determinism of that organism, group or species.

Axiom 83:   The self-determinism of an organism is determined by its THETA endowment, modified by minus or plus randomity in its environment or its existence.

Axiom 84:   The self-determinism of an organism is increased by optimum randomity of counter-efforts.

Axiom 85:   The self-determinism of an organism is reduced by plus or minus randomity of counter-efforts in the environment.

Axiom 86:   Randomity contains both the randomness of efforts and the volume of efforts. (Note: An area of randomity can have a great deal of confusion, but without volume of energy, the confusion itself is negligible.)

Axiom 87:   That counter-effort is most acceptable to an organism which most closely appears to assist its accomplishment of its goal.

Axiom 88:   An area of severe plus or minus randomity can occlude data on any of the subjects of that plus or minus *randomity which took place in a prior time. (Note: Shut-off mechanisms of earlier lives, perceptics, specific incidents, etc.)*

Axiom 89: *Restimulation of plus, minus or optimum randomity can produce increased plus, minus or optimum randomity respectively in the organism.*

Axiom 90: *An area of randomity can assume sufficient magnitude so as to appear to the organism as pain, according to its goals.*

Axiom 91: *Past randomity can impose itself upon the present organism as* THETA FACSIMILES.

Axiom 92: *The engram is a severe area of plus or minus randomity of sufficient volume to cause unconsciousness.*

Axiom 93: *Unconsciousness is an excess of randomity imposed by a counter-effort of sufficient force to cloud the awareness and direct function of the organism through the mind's control center.*

Axiom 94: *Any counter-effort which misaligns the organism's command of itself or its environment establishes plus or minus randomity or, if of sufficient magnitude, is an engram.*

Axiom 95: *Past engrams are restimulated by the control center's perception of circumstances similar to that engram in the present environment.*

Axiom 96: *An engram is a* THETA FACSIMILE *of atoms and molecules in misalignment.*

Axiom 97:   *Engrams fix emotional response as that emotional response of the organism during the receipt of the counter-effort.*

Axiom 98:   *Free emotional response depends on optimum randomity. It depends upon absence of or nonrestimulation of engrams.*

Axiom 99:   *THETA FACSIMILES can recombine into new symbols.*

Axiom 100:   *Language is the symbolization of effort.*

Axiom 101:   *Language depends for its force upon the force which accompanied its definition. (Note: Counter-effort, not language, is aberrative.)*

Axiom 102:   *The environment can occlude the central control of any organism and assume control of the motor controls of that organism. (Engram, restimulation, locks, hypnotism.)*

Axiom 103:   *Intelligence depends on the ability to select aligned or misaligned data from an area of randomity and so discover a solution to reduce all randomity in that area.*

Axiom 104:   *Persistence obtains in the ability of the mind to put solutions into physical action toward the realization of goals.*

Axiom 105:   *An unknown datum can produce data of plus or minus randomity.*

Axiom 106:   *The introduction of an arbitrary factor or force without recourse to natural laws of the body or the area into which the arbitrary is introduced brings about plus or minus randomity.*

Axiom 107: *Data of plus or minus randomity depends for its confusion on former plus or minus randomity or absent data.*

Axiom 108: *Efforts which are inhibited or compelled by exterior efforts effect a plus or minus randomity of efforts.*

Axiom 109: *Behavior is modified by counter-efforts which have impinged on the organism.*

Axiom 110: *The component parts of* THETA *are affinity, reality and communication.*

Axiom 111: *Self-determinism consists of maximal affinity, reality and communication.*

Axiom 112: *Affinity is the cohesion of* THETA.
Affinity manifests itself as the recognition of similarity of efforts and goals amongst organisms by those organisms.

Axiom 113: *Reality is the agreement upon perceptions and data in the physical universe.*
All that we can be sure is real is that on which we have agreed is real. Agreement is the essence of reality.

Axiom 114: *Communication is the interchange of perception through the material universe between organisms or the perception of the material universe by sense channels.*

Axiom 115: *Self-determinism is the* THETA *control of the organism.*

Axiom 116: *A self-determined effort is that counter-effort which has been received into the organism in the past and integrated into the organism for its conscious use.*

Axiom 117: The components of self-determinism are affinity, communication and reality.

Self-determinism is manifested along each dynamic.

Axiom 118: An organism cannot become aberrated unless it has agreed upon that aberration, has been in communication with a source of aberration and has had affinity for the aberrator.

Axiom 119: Agreement with any source, contra- or prosurvival, postulates a new reality for the organism.

Axiom 120: Nonsurvival courses, thoughts and actions require nonoptimum effort.

Axiom 121: Every thought has been preceded by physical action.

Axiom 122: The mind does with thought as it has done with entities in the physical universe.

Axiom 123: All effort concerned with pain is concerned with loss.

Organisms hold pain and engrams to them as a latent effort to prevent loss of some portion of the organism.

All loss is a loss of motion.

Axiom 124: The amount of counter-effort the organism can overcome is proportional to the THETA endowment of the organism, modified by the physique of that organism.

Axiom 125: Excessive counter-effort to the effort of a life organism produces unconsciousness.

COROLLARY: Unconsciousness gives the suppression of an organism's control center by counter-effort.

DEFINITION: The control center of the organism can be defined as the contact point between THETA and the physical universe and is that center which is aware of being aware and which has charge of and responsibility for the organism along all its dynamics.

Axiom 126: Perceptions are always received in the control center of an organism whether the control center is in control of the organism at the time or not.
This is an explanation for the assumption of valences.

Axiom 127: All perceptions reaching the organism's sense channels are recorded and stored by THETA FACSIMILE.
DEFINITION: Perception is the process of recording data from the physical universe and storing it as a THETA FACSIMILE.
DEFINITION: Recall is the process of regaining perceptions.

Axiom 128: Any organism can recall everything which it has perceived.

Axiom 129: An organism displaced by plus or minus randomity is thereafter remote from the perception recording center.
Increased remoteness brings about occlusions of perceptions. One can perceive things in present time and then, because they are being recorded after they passed THETA perception of the awareness unit, they are recorded but cannot be recalled.

Axiom 130: THETA FACSIMILES of counter-effort are all that interpose between the control center and its recalls.

Axiom 131: Any counter-effort received into a control center is always accompanied by all perceptics.

Axiom 132: The random counter-efforts to an organism and the intermingled perceptions in the randomity can reexert that force upon an organism when restimulated.
DEFINITION: Restimulation is the reactivation of a past counter-effort by appearance in the organism's environment of a similarity toward the content of the past randomity area.

Axiom 133: Self-determinism alone brings about the mechanism of restimulation.

Axiom 134: A reactivated area of the past randomity impinges the effort and the perceptions upon the organism.

Axiom 135: Activation of a randomity area is accomplished first by the perceptions, then by the pain, finally by the effort.

Axiom 136: The mind is plastically capable of recording all efforts and counter-efforts.

Axiom 137: A counter-effort accompanied by sufficient (enrandomed) force impresses the facsimile of the counter-effort personality into the mind of an organism.

Axiom 138: Aberration is the degree of residual plus or minus randomity accumulated by compelling, inhibiting or unwarranted assisting of efforts on the part of other organisms or the physical (material) universe.
Aberration is caused by what is done to the individual, not what the individual does, plus his self-determinism about what has been done to him.

Axiom 139: *Aberrated behavior consists of destructive effort toward prosurvival data or entities on any dynamic, or effort toward the survival of contrasurvival data or entities for any dynamic.*

Axiom 140: *A valence is a facsimile personality made capable of force by the counter-effort of the moment of receipt into the plus or minus randomity of unconsciousness.*
Valences are assistive, compulsive or inhibitive to the organism.
A control center is not a valence.

Axiom 141: *A control center effort is aligned toward a goal through definite space as a recognized incident in time.*

Axiom 142: *An organism is as healthy and sane as it is self-determined.*
The environmental control of the organism motor controls inhibits the organism's ability to change with the changing environment, since the organism will attempt to carry forward with one set of responses when it needs by self-determinism to create another to survive in another environment.

Axiom 143: *All learning is accomplished by random effort.*

Axiom 144: *A counter-effort producing sufficient plus or minus randomity to record is recorded with an index of space and time as hidden as the remainder of its content.*

Axiom 145: *A counter-effort producing sufficient plus or minus randomity when activated by restimulation exerts itself against the environment or the organism without regard to space and time, except reactivated perceptions.*

Axiom 146: *Counter-efforts are directed out from the organism until they are further enrandomed by the environ at which time they again activate against the control center.*

Axiom 147: *An organism's mind employs counter-efforts effectively only so long as insufficient plus or minus randomity exists to hide differentiation of the facsimiles created.*

Axiom 148: *Physical laws are learned by life energy only by impingement of the physical universe producing randomity, and a withdrawal from that impingement.*

Axiom 149: *Life depends upon an alignment of force vectors in the direction of survival and the nullification of force vectors in the direction of succumb in order to survive.*
COROLLARY: Life depends upon an alignment of force vectors in the direction of succumb and the nullification of force vectors in the direction of survive in order to succumb.

Axiom 150: *Any area of randomity gathers to it situations similar to it which do not contain actual efforts but only perceptions.*

Axiom 151: *Whether an organism has the goal of surviving or succumbing depends upon the amount of plus or minus randomity it has reactivated. (Not residual.)*

Axiom 152: *Survival is accomplished only by motion.*

Axiom 153: *In the physical universe the absence of motion is vanishment.*

Axiom 154: *Death is the equivalent to life of total lack of life-motivated motion.*

Axiom 155: *Acquisition of prosurvival matter and energy or organisms in space and time means increased motion.*

Axiom 156: *Loss of prosurvival matter and energy or organisms in space and time means decreased motion.*

Axiom 157: *Acquisition or proximity of matter, energy or organisms which assist the survival of an organism increase the survival potentials of an organism.*

Axiom 158: *Acquisition or proximity of matter, energy or organisms which inhibit the survival of an organism decrease its survival potential.*

Axiom 159: *Gain of survival energy, matter or organisms increases the freedom of an organism.*

Axiom 160: *Receipt or proximity of nonsurvival energy, matter or time decreases the freedom of motion of an organism.*

Axiom 161: *The control center attempts the halting or lengthening of time, the expansion or contraction of space and the decrease or increase of energy and matter.*
This is a primary source of invalidation, and it is also a primary source of aberration.

Axiom 162: *Pain is the balk of effort by counter-effort in great intensity, whether that effort is to remain at rest or in motion.*

Axiom 163: *Perception, including pain, can be exhausted from an area of plus or minus randomity, still leaving the effort and counter-effort of that plus or minus randomity.*

Axiom 164: *The rationality of the mind depends upon an optimum reaction toward time.*
DEFINITION: Sanity, the computation of futures.
DEFINITION: Neurotic, the computation of present time only.
DEFINITION: Psychotic, computation only of past situations.

Axiom 165: *Survival pertains only to the future.*
COROLLARY: Succumb pertains only to the present and past.

Axiom 166: *An individual is as happy as he can perceive survival potentials in the future.*

Axiom 167: *As the needs of any organism are met it rises higher and higher in its efforts along the dynamics.*
An organism which achieves ARC with itself can better achieve ARC with sex in the future; having achieved this it can achieve ARC with groups; having achieved this, it can achieve ARC with mankind, etc.

Axiom 168: *Affinity, reality and communication coexist in an inextricable relationship.*
The coexistent relationship between affinity, reality and communication is such that none can be increased without increasing the other two and none can be decreased without decreasing the other two.

Axiom 169: *Any aesthetic product is a symbolic facsimile or combination of facsimiles of THETA or physical universes in varied randomities and volumes of randomities with the interplay of tones.*

Axiom 170: *An aesthetic product is an interpretation of the universes by an individual or group mind.*

Axiom 171: Delusion is the postulation by the imagination of occurrences in areas of plus or minus randomity.

Axiom 172: Dreams are the imaginative reconstruction of areas of randomity or the resymbolization of the efforts of THETA.

Axiom 173: A motion is created by the degree of optimum randomity introduced by the counter-effort to an organism's effort.

Axiom 174: MEST which has been mobilized by life forms is in more affinity with life organisms than nonmobilized MEST.

Axiom 175: All past perception, conclusion and existence moments, including those of plus or minus randomity, are recoverable to the control center of the organism.

Axiom 176: The ability to produce survival effort on the part of an organism is affected by the degrees of randomity existing in its past. (This includes learning.)

Axiom 177: Areas of past plus or minus randomity can be readdressed by the control center of an organism and the plus or minus randomity exhausted.

Axiom 178: The exhaustion of past plus or minus randomities permits the control center of an organism to effect its own efforts toward survival goals.

Axiom 179: The exhaustion of self-determined effort from a past area of plus or minus randomity nullifies the effectiveness of that area.

Axiom 180: Pain is the randomity produced by sudden or strong counter-efforts.

Axiom 181: *Pain is stored as plus or minus randomity.*

Axiom 182: *Pain, as an area of plus or minus randomity, can reinflict itself upon the organism.*

Axiom 183: *Past pain becomes ineffective upon the organism when the randomity of its area is addressed and aligned.*

Axiom 184: *The earlier the area of plus or minus randomity, the greater self-produced effort existed to repel it.*

Axiom 185: *Later areas of plus or minus randomity cannot be realigned easily until earlier areas are realigned.*

Axiom 186: *Areas of plus or minus randomity become increased in activity when perceptions of similarity are introduced into them.*

Axiom 187: *Past areas of plus or minus randomity can be reduced and aligned by address to them in present time.*

Axiom 188: *Absolute good and absolute evil do not exist in the MEST universe.*

Axiom 189: *That which is good for an organism may be defined as that which promotes the survival of that organism.*
CoROLLARY: Evil may be defined as that which inhibits or brings plus or minus randomity into the organism, which is contrary to the survival motives of the organism.

Axiom 190: *Happiness consists in the act of bringing alignment into hitherto resisting plus or minus randomity. Neither the act or action of attaining survival, nor the accomplishment of this act itself, brings about happiness.*

Axiom 191: *Construction is an alignment of data.*
COROLLARY: Destruction is a plus or minus randomity of data.
The effort of constructing is the alignment toward the survival of the aligning organism.
Destruction is the effort of bringing randomity into an area.

Axiom 192: *Optimum survival behavior consists of effort in the maximum survival interest in everything concerned in the dynamics.*

Axiom 193: *The optimum survival solution of any problem would consist of the highest attainable survival for every dynamic concerned.*

Axiom 194: *The worth of any organism consists of its value to the survival of its own THETA along any dynamic.*

About the Author

L. Ron Hubbard is one of the most acclaimed and widely read authors of all time, primarily because his works express a firsthand knowledge of the nature of man—knowledge gained not from standing on the sidelines but through lifelong experience with people from all walks of life.

As Ron said, "One doesn't learn about life by sitting in an ivory tower, thinking about it. One learns about life by being part of it." And that is how he lived.

He began his quest for knowledge on the nature of man at a very early age. When he was eight years old he was already well on his way to being a seasoned traveler, covering a quarter of a million miles by the age of nineteen. His adventures included voyages to China, Japan and other points in the Orient and South Pacific. During this time he became closely acquainted with twenty-one different races in areas all over the world.

After returning to the United States, Ron pursued his formal studies of mathematics and engineering at George Washington University, where he was also a member of one of the first classes on nuclear physics. He realized that neither the East nor the West contained the full answer to the problems of existence.

Despite all of mankind's advances in the physical sciences, a *workable* technology of the mind and life had never been developed. The mental "technologies" which did exist, psychology and psychiatry, were actually barbaric, false subjects—no more workable than the methods of jungle witch doctors. Ron shouldered the responsibility of filling this gap in the knowledge of mankind.

He financed his early research through fiction writing. He became one of the most highly demanded authors in the golden age of popular adventure and science fiction writing during the 1930s and 1940s, interrupted only by his service in the U.S. Navy during World War II.

Partially disabled at the war's end, Ron applied what he had learned from his research. He made breakthroughs and developed techniques which made it possible for him to recover from his injuries and help others to regain their health. It was during this time that the basic tenets of Dianetics technology were codified.

A year later, in 1948, he wrote the first manuscript detailing his discoveries. Ron did not have it published at that time, but gave copies to some friends who copied it and passed among their friends who then passed it on to others. (This book was formally published in 1951 as *Dianetics: The Original Thesis* and later republished as *The Dynamics of Life*.) The interest generated by this manuscript prompted a flood of requests for more information on the subject.

Ron attempted to make all his discoveries available to the American Psychiatric Association and the American Medical Association. Despite the fact that his work would have benefited them and thereby society immensely, his offers were refused. These same vested interests decided that Dianetics could harm their profits (which were and still are based on the amount of illness and insanity in our culture) and began to attack Ron and his work. He therefore decided to write a comprehensive text on the subject and take it directly to the public.

With the publication of *Dianetics: The Modern Science of Mental Health* on May 9, 1950, a complete handbook for the application of Ron's new technology was broadly available for the first time. *Dianetics* created a wildfire of public interest. The book immediately shot to the top of the New York Times bestseller list and stayed there week after week. More than 750 Dianetics study groups sprang up within a few short months of its publication.

Ron kept on researching, improving methods and developing ways to advance other people's ability to apply Dianetics technology.

One of his breakthroughs resulted in *Self Analysis*, a book by which a person could be in better communication with himself and his world. The technique enhances memory and increases a person's ability to work with his own mind.

However, Ron's work advanced very rapidly, and less than a year later he had made new discoveries that led to a much more comprehensive process: Advanced Procedure, a series of actions that involved handling the person's own basic considerations and postulates. From Advanced Procedure Ron developed a second self-help work, by which he, through the medium of a book, could process an almost unlimited number of preclears. This was *Handbook for Preclears*, the self-help companion volume to *Advanced Procedure and Axioms*.

Ron's work did not stop with the successes of Dianetics. Further research led him to the basic truths of life itself and from these discoveries he developed Scientology, the first totally workable technology for the improvement of life.

The number of books and lectures continued to grow for more than three decades as Ron kept on with his research into the mind and life.

Today Ron's works—including an astounding number of books, taped lectures, instructional films, writings, demonstrations and briefings—are studied and applied daily. Dianetics and Scientology techniques are used in hundreds of Hubbard Dianetics Foundations and Scientology organizations on every continent.

With his research fully completed and codified, L. Ron Hubbard departed his body on January 24, 1986.

Ron's work opened a new door for mankind. Through his efforts, there now exists a totally workable technology with which people can help each other improve their lives and succeed in achieving their goals.

Millions of people all over the world consider they have no truer friend.

Glossary

Aberration: a departure from rational thought or behavior. From the Latin, *aberrare,* to wander from; Latin, *ab,* away, *errare,* to wander. It means basically to err, to make mistakes, or more specifically to have fixed ideas which are not true. Aberration is opposed to sanity, which would be its opposite.

Act: a stage of auditing. Applies solely to the particular process in use at a certain case level.

adept: a skilled or proficient person; expert.

anthropoid: any tailless ape of the families Pongidae and Hylobatidae, anatomically resembling humans, and comprising the gorillas, chimpanzees, orangutans, gibbons and siamangs.

anthropologist: one who specializes in anthropology, the science that deals with the origins, physical and cultural development, biological characteristics and social customs and beliefs of humankind.

appendage: a subordinate part attached to something; an auxiliary part; addition.

assessment: an inventory, an examination, a calculation or evaluation of a case.

auditing: the application of Dianetics processes and procedures to someone by a trained auditor. The exact definition of auditing is: The action of asking a person a question (which he can understand and answer), getting an answer to that question and acknowledging him for that answer.

auditor: a person trained and qualified in applying Dianetics processes and procedures to individuals for their betterment; called an auditor because *auditor* means *one who listens.*

biologist: a specialist in biology, the science of life or living matter in all its forms and phenomena, especially with reference to origin, growth, reproduction, structure and behavior.

blueprint: any pattern or model; template.

catalyst: a person or thing which precipitates an event or change.

chary: cautious or careful; wary.

Clear: the name of a state achieved through auditing or an individual who has achieved this state. A Clear is a being who no longer has his own reactive mind. A Clear is an unaberrated person and is rational in that he forms the best possible solutions he can on the data he has and from his viewpoint. The Clear has no engrams which can be restimulated to throw out the correctness of computation by entering hidden and false data.

cohesion: (physics) the molecular force between particles within a body or substance that acts to unite them.

collectivism: the political principle of centralized social and economic control, especially of all means of production.

corn: referring to the practice of ancient Rome of feeding people and providing official public amusement (circuses in the arena) in order to prevent unrest. Also known as "bread and circuses."

corollary: a proposition that is incidentally proved in proving another proposition.

crustaceans: animals with a hard shell, jointed body and appendages and gills that live mostly in water. Crabs, lobsters and shrimp are crustaceans.

Doppler effect: the shift in frequency of acoustic or electromagnetic radiation emitted by a source moving relative to the observer as seen by the observer: the shift is to higher frequencies when the source approaches and to lower frequencies when it recedes.

effort: the physical force manifestation of motion. A sharp effort against an individual produces pain. A strenuous effort produces discomfort. Effort can be recalled and reexperienced by the preclear.

Einstein: Albert Einstein (1879–1955), German physicist, US citizen from 1940, formulator of the theory of relativity.

endocrine: pertaining to any of the various glands, as the thyroid, adrenal and pituitary glands, that secrete certain substances or hormones directly into the blood or lymph.

endocrinologists: specialists in the field of endocrinology, the branch of biology that deals with the anatomy and function of the endocrine glands, such as the thyroid, adrenal and pituitary glands, which secrete certain substances or hormones directly into the blood or lymph.

endowment: a gift of nature.

ethereal: light, airy or tenuous.

facetiously: in a manner not meant to be taken seriously or literally.

faculty: an ability, natural or acquired, for a particular kind of action.

feign: make a false show of; pretend; imitate.

Field, Eugene: (1850–95) American poet and journalist, best known as poet of children's verse.

game leg: lame or injured leg.

genetic: by line of protoplasm and by facsimiles and by MEST forms the individual has arrived in the present age from a past beginning. Genetic applies to the protoplasm line of father and mother to child, grown child to new child and so forth.

Genghis Khan: (1162–1227) Mongol conqueror of most of Asia and of east Europe to the Dnieper River.

Gibbon: Edward Gibbon (1737–94). English historian whose chief work was *The History of the Decline and Fall of the Roman Empire.*

glandular: having to do with glands, any organ or specialized group of cells that separates certain elements from the blood and secretes them in a form for the body to use, as epinephrine, or throw off, as urine or sweat.

Halley: Edmund Halley (1656–1742), English astronomer. Best known for his study of comets.

heroically: in an extreme manner.

humbuggery: pretense; sham.

impedance: something that obstructs or hinders.

inertia: a tendency to remain in a fixed condition without change; disinclination to move or act.

irregular: a soldier or combatant not of a regular military force, such as a guerrilla or "freedom fighter."

Krag-Jorgenson: Norwegian-designed rifle used by US forces at the turn of the century.

libido theories: theories like that of Sigmund Freud's which states that all life impulses and behavior are sex-motivated.

Little Nell: character in the novel *The Old Curiosity Shop* by Charles Dickens (1812–70, English).

Little Orphan Annie: character in a comic strip of the same name.

marauder: a person or animal who goes around in search of plunder.

mollusk: any one of a large group of animals having no backbone, soft bodies not composed of segments, and usually covered with a hard shell of one or more parts. The shell of mollusks is secreted by a covering mantle and is formed on snails, clams, oysters, whelks and mussels. Slugs, octopuses and squids have no shell. Mollusks make up a phylum in the animal kingdom.

moth-chewed: same as *moth-eaten*: out of fashion; antiquated.

Newton: Isaac Newton (1642–1727), English mathematician and natural philosopher, formulator of the laws of gravity and motion.

onerous: burdensome, oppressive or troublesome; causing hardship.

orthodox: customary or conventional, as a means or method; established.

ostracized: exluded, by general consent, from society, friend- ship, conversation, privileges, etc.

Paul, St.: (died about 67 A.D.) an early Christian missionary who started Christian communities in many countries and wrote most of the epistles in the New Testament.

plaint: a complaint.

plastic: pliable; impressionable.

polio: an acute viral disease, usually affecting children and young adults, caused by any of three polioviruses, charac- terized by inflammation of the motor neurons of the brain stem and spinal cord, and resulting in a motor paralysis, followed by muscular atrophy and often permanent defor- mities.

postulated: made a decision to yourself or others.

preclear: a spiritual being who is now on the road to becoming Clear, hence pre-Clear.

privation: lack of the ordinary necessities or comforts of life.

psychotic: an individual who is out of contact to a thorough extent with his present-time environment and who does not compute into the future. He may be an acute psychotic wherein he becomes psychotic for only a few minutes at a time and only occasionally in certain environments (as in rages or apathies) or he may be a chronic psychotic, or in a continual disconnection with the future and present. Psy- chotics who are dramatically harmful to others are consid- ered dangerous enough to be put away. Psychotics who are harmful on a less dramatic basis are no less harmful to their environment and are no less psychotic.

release: (verb) the act of taking the perceptions or effort or effectiveness out of a heavy facsimile or taking away the preclear's hold on the facsimile.

remission: a relatively prolonged lessening or disappearance of the symptoms of a disease.

resilience: ability to recover readily from illness, depression, adversity or the like.

saline content: salt content.

servomechanism: an electronic control system in which a hydraulic, pneumatic or other type of controlling mechanism is actuated and controlled by a low-energy signal.

shamans: (especially among certain tribal peoples) persons who act as intermediaries between the natural and supernatural worlds, using magic to cure illness, foretell the future, control spiritual forces, etc.

sinusitis: an inflammation of a sinus or the sinuses.

sloth: a very slow-moving mammal of South or Central America that lives in trees.

sordid: degraded.

Standard Procedure: a set of exact steps used by an auditor in auditing a preclear.

statics: things which have no mass, no location and no position in time, and which have no wavelength at all.

tarsus: tarsier: any one of a genus of small, nocturnal primates of

Indonesia and the Philippines, with wide eyes and long, bare tails.

Tiny Tim: character from the novel *A Christmas Carol* by Charles Dickens (1812–70, English).

transient: not lasting, enduring or permanent.

transits: instruments used in surveying to measure horizontal and vertical angles.

whooping cough: an infectious disease, usually of children, that causes fits of coughing that end with a loud, gasping sound (whoop).

Index

Books and Tapes
by L. Ron Hubbard

Dianetics Graduate Books

You've read *Handbook for Preclears*. Now get the rest of the Dianetics Graduate Books Package. These books by L. Ron Hubbard give you detailed knowledge of how the mind works—data you can use to help yourself and others break out of the traps of life. While you can get these books individually, the Dianetics Graduate Books Package can also be purchased as a set, complete with an attractive slipcase.

Science of Survival • If you ever wondered how people act the way they do, you'll find this book a wealth of information. It's vital to anyone who wants to understand others and improve personal relationships. *Science of Survival* is built around a remarkable chart—The Hubbard Chart of Human Evaluation. With it you can understand and predict other people's behavior and reactions and greatly increase your control over your own life. This is a valuable handbook that can make a difference between success and failure on the job and in life.

Dianetics 55! • Your success in life depends on your ability to communicate. Do you know a formula exists for communication? Learn the rules of better communication that can help you live a more fulfilling life. Here, L. Ron Hubbard deals with the fundamental principles of communication and how you can master these to achieve your goals.

Advanced Procedure and Axioms • For the *first* time the basics of thought and the physical universe have been codified into a set of fundamental laws, signaling an entirely new way to view and approach the subjects of man, the physical universe and even life itself.

Child Dianetics • Here is a revolutionary new approach to rearing children with Dianetics auditing techniques. Find out how you can help your child achieve greater confidence, more self-reliance, improved learning rate and a happier, more loving relationship with you.

Notes on the Lectures of L. Ron Hubbard • Compiled from his fascinating lectures given shortly after the publication of *Dianetics*, this book contains some of the first material Ron ever released on the ARC Triangle and the Tone Scale, and how these discoveries relate to auditing.

Basic Dianetics Books

The Basic Dianetics Books Package is your complete guide to the inner workings of the mind. You can get all of these books individually or in a set, complete with an attractive slipcase.

Dianetics: The Modern Science of Mental Health • Acclaimed as the most effective self-help book ever published. Dianetics technology has helped millions reach new heights of freedom and ability. Millions of copies are sold every year! Discover the source of mental barriers that prevent you from achieving your goals—and how to handle them!

The Dynamics of Life • Break through the barriers to your happiness. This is the first book Ron wrote detailing the startling principles behind Dianetics—facts so powerful they can change forever the way you look at yourself and your potentials. Discover how you can use the powerful basic principles in this book to blast through the barriers of your mind and gain full control over your success, future and happiness.

Self Analysis • The complete do-it-yourself handbook for anyone who wants to improve their abilities and success potential. Use the simple, easy-to-learn techniques in *Self Analysis* to build self-confidence and reduce stress.

Dianetics: The Evolution of a Science • It is estimated that we use less than ten percent of our mind's potential. What stops us from developing and using the full potential of our minds? *Dianetics: The Evolution of a Science* is L. Ron Hubbard's incredible story of how he discovered the reactive mind and how he developed the keys to unlock its secrets. Get this firsthand account of what the mind really is, and how you can release its hidden potential.

Basic Scientology Books

The Basic Scientology Books Package contains the knowledge you need to be able to improve conditions in life. These books are available individually or as a set, complete with an attractive slipcase.

Scientology: The Fundamentals of Thought • Improve life *and* make a better world with this easy-to-read book that lays out the fundamental truths about life and thought. No such knowledge has ever before existed, and no such results have ever before been attainable as those which can be reached by the use of this knowledge. Equipped with this book alone, one could perform seeming miracles in changing the states of health, ability and intelligence of people. This *is* how life works. This *is* how you change men, women and children for the better, and attain greater personal freedom.

A New Slant on Life • Have you ever asked yourself who am I? What am I? This book of articles by L. Ron Hubbard answers these all too common questions. This is knowledge one can use every day—for a new, more confident and happier slant on life!

The Problems of Work • Work plays a big part in the game of life. Do you really enjoy your work? Are you certain of your job security? Would you like the increased personal satisfaction of doing your work well? This is the book that shows exactly how to achieve these things and more. The game of life—and within it, the game of work—can be enjoyable and rewarding.

Scientology 0-8: The Book of Basics • What is life? Did you know an individual can create space, energy and time? Here are the basics of life itself, and the secrets of becoming cause over any area of your life. Discover how you can use the data in this book to achieve your goals.

Basic Dictionary of Dianetics and Scientology • Compiled from the works of L. Ron Hubbard, this convenient dictionary contains the terms and expressions needed by anyone learning Dianetics and Scientology technology. And a *special bonus*—an easy-to-read Scientology Organizing Board chart that shows you who to contact for services and information at your nearest Scientology Organization.

OT Library Package

All the following books contain the knowledge of a spiritual being's relationship to this universe and how his abilities to operate successfully in it can be restored. You can get all of these books individually or in a set, complete with an attractive slipcase.

Scientology 8-80 • What are the laws of life? We are all familiar with physical laws such as the law of gravity, but what laws govern life and thought? L. Ron Hubbard answers the riddles of life and its goals in the physical universe.

Scientology 8-8008 • Get the basic truths about your nature as a spiritual being and your relationship to the physical universe around you. Here, L. Ron Hubbard describes procedures designed to greatly increase your abilities and the power of your own universe.

Scientology: A History of Man • A fascinating look at the evolutionary background and history of the human race. This was Ron's first book on the vast time track of man. As Ron said, "This is a cold-blooded and factual account of your last sixty trillion years."

The Creation of Human Ability • This book contains processes designed to restore the power of a thetan over his own postulates, to understand the nature of his beingness, to free his self-determinism and much, much more.

The Phoenix Lectures • Containing L. Ron Hubbard's most complete discussion of the Scientology Axioms, *The Phoenix Lectures* gives you the full knowledge of the basic agreements which make up the very nature of the universe we live in.

The E-Meter Books Package

The following books on the E-Meter give all the data you need to understand and professionally operate your E-Meter. You can get all of these books individually or in a set, complete with an attractive slipcase.

Introducing the E-Meter • This is a basic book that introduces you to the E-Meter spiritual counseling device and its operation.

Understanding the E-Meter • A large, illustrated book that fully explains the basics of the E-Meter device, how it works and how it can measure the electrical activity of thought. Any question on the principles of the E-Meter can be answered with this book.

E-Meter Essentials • This book gives more advanced aspects of E-Meter use, plus a detailed description of the different types of meter reads on the meter and what they mean.

The Book of E-Meter Drills • With this book you learn all phases of E-Meter operation with detailed, hands-on drills.

Other Scientology Books

Purification: An Illustrated Answer to Drugs • Do toxins and drugs hold down your ability to think clearly? What is the Purification Program and how does it work? How can harmful chemical substances be gotten out of the body? Our society is ridden by abuse of drugs, alcohol and medicine that reduce one's ability to think clearly. Find out what can be done in this introduction to the Purification Program.

All About Radiation • Can the effects of radiation exposure be avoided or reduced? What exactly would happen in the event of an atomic explosion? Get the answers to these and many other questions in this illuminating book. *All About Radiation* describes observations and discoveries concerning the physical and mental effects of radiation and the possibilities for handling them. Get the real facts on the subject of radiation and its effects.

Have You Lived Before This Life? • This is the book that sparked a flood of interest in the ancient puzzle: Does man live only one life? The answer lay in mystery, buried until L. Ron Hubbard's researches unearthed the truth. Actual case histories of people recalling past lives in auditing tell the tale.

Mission Into Time • Here is a fascinating account of a unique research expedition into both space and time, locating physical evidence of past lives in an area rich with history—the Mediterranean. Read Ron's story of the exploration of locations recalled from previous lives!

Dianetics and Scientology Technical Dictionary • This dictionary is your indispensable guide to the words and ideas of Scientology and Dianetics technologies—technologies which can help you increase your know-how and effectiveness in life. Over three thousand words are defined—including a new understanding of vital words like *life, love* and *happiness* as well as Scientology terms.

Modern Management Technology Defined: Hubbard Dictionary of Administration and Management • Here's a real breakthrough in the subject of administration and management! Eighty-six hundred words are defined for greater understanding of any business situation. Clear, precise Scientology definitions describe many previously baffling phenomena and bring truth, sanity and understanding to the often murky field of business management.

How to Live Though an Executive • What are the factors in business and commerce which, if lacking, can keep a person overworked and worried, keep labor and management at each other's throats, and make an unsafe working atmosphere? L. Ron Hubbard reveals principles based on years of research into many different types of organizations.

Introduction to Scientology Ethics • A complete knowledge of ethics is vital to anyone's success in life. Without knowing and applying the information in this book, success is only a matter of luck or chance. That is not much to look forward to. This book contains the answers to questions like, "How do I know when a decision is right or wrong?" "How can I predictably improve things around me?" The powerful ethics technology of L. Ron Hubbard is your way to ever-increasing survival.

Organization Executive Course • The *Organization Executive Course* volumes contain organizational technology never before known to man. This is not just how a Scientology organization works; this is how the operation of *any* organization, *any* activity, can be improved. A person knowing the data in these volumes fully, and applying it, could completely reverse any downtrend in a company—or even a country!

Management Series Volume 1 and 2 • These books contain technology that anyone who works with management in any way must know completely to be a true success. Contained in these books are such subjects as data evaluation, the technology of how to organize any area for maximum production and expansion, how to handle personnel, the actual technology of public relations and much more.

Background and Ceremonies of the Church of Scientology • Discover the beautiful and inspiring ceremonies of the Church of Scientology, and its fascinating religious and historical background. This book contains the illuminating Creed of the Church, church services, sermons and ceremonies, many as originally given in person by L. Ron Hubbard, Founder of Scientology.

What Is Scientology? • Scientology applied religious philosophy has attracted great interest and attention since its beginning. What is Scientology philosophy? What can it accomplish— and why are so many people from all walks of life proclaiming its effectiveness? Find the answers to these questions and many others in *What Is Scientology?*

Introductory and Demonstration Processes and Assists • How can you help someone increase his enthusiasm for living?

How can you improve someone's self-confidence on the job? Here are basic Scientology processes you can use to help others deal with life and living.

Volunteer Minister's Handbook • This is a big, practical how-to-do-it book to give a person the basic knowledge on how to help self and others through the rough spots in life. It consists of twenty-one sections—each one covering important situations in life, such as drug and alcohol problems, study difficulties, broken marriages, accidents and illnesses, a failing business, difficult children, and much more. This is the basic tool you need to help someone out of troubles, and bring about a happier life.

Research and Discovery Series • These volumes contain that only existing day-to-day, week-to-week record of the progress of L. Ron Hubbard's research in Dianetics and Scientology. Through the pages of these beautiful volumes you follow L. Ron Hubbard's fantastic research adventure, beginning in the depths of man's degradation and obsession with the material universe and soaring to the realms of the spirit, freed from the bondage of the past.

Technical Bulletins • These volumes contain all of L. Ron Hubbard's technical bulletins and issues from the earliest to the latest. Almost any technical question can be answered from the pages of these volumes, which also include an extremely extensive master subject index.

The Classic Cassettes Series

There are nearly three thousand recorded lectures by L. Ron Hubbard on the subjects of Dianetics and Scientology. What follows is a sampling of these lectures, each known and loved the world over. All of the Classic Cassettes are presented in Clearsound state-of-the-art sound-recording technology, notable for its clarity and brilliance of reproduction.

The Story of Dianetics and Scientology • In this lecture, L. Ron Hubbard shares with you his earliest insights into human nature and gives a compelling and often humorous account of his experiences. Spend an unforgettable time with Ron as he talks about the start of Dianetics and Scientology!

The Road to Truth • The road to truth has eluded man since the beginning of time. In this classic lecture, L. Ron Hubbard explains what this road actually is and why it is the only road one MUST travel all the way once begun. This lecture reveals the only road to higher levels of living.

Scientology and Effective Knowledge • Voyage to new horizons of awareness! *Scientology and Effective Knowledge* by L. Ron Hubbard can help you understand more about yourself and others. A fascinating tale of the beginnings of Dianetics and Scientology.

The Deterioration of Liberty • What do governments fear so much in a population that they amass weapons to defend themselves from people? Find out from Ron in this classic lecture.

Man's Relentless Search • Learn about man's search for himself and his true nature. Find out where this search led and how through Ron's work we have achieved a knowledge of man's true self.

Power of Choice and Self-Determinism • Man's ability to determine the course of his life depends on his ability to exercise his power of choice. Find how you can increase your power of choice and self-determinism in life from Ron in this lecture.

Scientology and Ability • Ron points out that this universe is here because we perceive it and agree to it. Applying Scientology principles to life can bring new adventure to life and put you on the road to discovering better beingness.

The Road to Perfection • Find out what perfection really is and how Scientology gives you the means to attain it.

The Hope of Man • Various men in history brought forth the idea that there was hope of improvement. But L. Ron Hubbard's discoveries in Dianetics and Scientology have made that hope a reality. Find out by listening to this lecture how Scientology has become man's one, true hope for his final freedom.

The Dynamics • In this lecture Ron gives incredible data on the dynamics: how man creates on them, what happens when a person gets stuck in just one; how wars relate to the third dynamic and much more.

Health and Certainty • Ron talks in this classic lecture about the effect false certainty can bring about in an individual and how real certainty is achieved.

Miracles • What are miracles? How do they come about? Find out how things that used to pass as miracles have become just the expected results of Dianetics and Scientology.

My Philosophy • Three dramatic essays by Ron—"My Philosophy," "The Aims of Scientology" and "A Description of Scientology"—come alive for you in this cassette. These powerful writings, beautifully read and set to new and inspiring music, tell you what Scientology is, what it does and what its aims are.

More advanced books and lectures are available. Contact your nearest organization or write directly to the publisher for a full catalog.

Improve Your Life
with Dianetics Graduate
Extension Courses

Dianetics Graduate books by L. Ron Hubbard give you the knowledge of how the mind works and how you can use that data to help yourself and others to break out of the traps of life. The Dianetics Graduate Extension courses enable you to increase your application of the information contained in L. Ron Hubbard's books and make this a saner world for all.

Each extension course package includes a lesson book with easy-to-understand instructions and all the lessons you will need to complete it. Each course can be done in the comfort of your own home or right in your local Scientology organization. Your Extension Course Supervisor will review each lesson as you complete it (or mail it in if you do the course at home) and get the results right back to you. When you complete the course you get a beautiful certificate, suitable for framing.

Handbook for Preclears Extension Course

L. Ron Hubbard wrote this book in 1951 in response the need for an advanced personal workbook. People who follow the exact steps laid out in this book achieve definite, positive changes in the conditions in their lives. Find out what you CAN do about the conditions in your life. Enroll on the *Handbook for Preclears Extension Course* today!

Dianetics 55! Extension Course

Dianetics 55! forms an excellent bridge from the study of the mind to the study of knowledge in its fullest sense—Scientology. Doing the extension course for this book can help you grasp the tremendous amount of important data it contains so you can better apply this information to your benefit.

Science of Survival Extension Course

Science of Survival was written around a remarkable chart that lays out all the characteristics of human behavior—the Hubbard Chart of Human Evaluation. To learn more about what lies behind the emotional tone levels of others, how you predict how they will react and how to handle them, do the *Science of Survival Extension Course!*

Advanced Procedure and Axioms Extension Course

For the *first* time the basics of thought and the physical universe have been codified into a set of fundamental laws, signaling an entirely new way to view and approach the subjects of man, the physical universe and even life itself. Gain a full understanding of postulates, self-determinism and *full* responsibility on the *Advanced Procedure and Axioms Extension Course.*

Child Dianetics Extension Course

In 1951 Ron wrote in the introduction to *Child Dianetics*:
"The American Medical Association lately came out with a pamphlet which was called 'How to Control Your Child.' That's just what you don't want to do."
There *is* a correct way to have a successful relationship with children. Enroll on the *Child Dianetics Extension Course* and learn the workable way to get healthy, happier and more successful children. A "must" for any parent or teacher.

The Notes on the Lectures Extension Course

The physical universe and the universe of thought are two different universes that can have profound effects on an individual's ability to survive or succumb. Learn how Dianetics processing works to bring a person up out of the turbulence of the physical universe to the point of being able to create in life, on all Dynamics. Find out more about people—why they are what they are.

Enroll on a Dianetics Graduate Extension Course Today!

For information and enrollment and prices for these Extension Courses and the books they accompany, contact the Public Registrar at your nearest Church of Scientology. (A complete list of Scientology Churches and Organizations is provided at the back of this book.)

Get and start a Dianetics Graduate Extension Course today!

Get Your Free Catalog of Knowledge on How to Improve Life

L. Ron Hubbard's books and tapes increase your ability to understand yourself and others. His works give you the practical know-how you need to improve your life and the lives of your family and friends.

Many more materials by L. Ron Hubbard are available than have been covered in the pages of this book. A free catalog of these materials is available on request.

Write for your free catalog today!

Bridge Publications, Inc.
4751 Fountain Avenue
Los Angeles, California 90029

New Era Publications International, ApS
Store Kongensgade 55
1264 Copenhagen K, Denmark

Apply for Your International Association Membership Today!

The recently created International Association of Scientologists invites you to apply for your annual or lifetime membership today.

The purpose of the International Association of Scientologists is:

"to unite, advance, support and protect Scientology and Scientologists in all parts of the world so as to achieve the aims and purposes of Scientology."

Benefits extended to International Association members include:

* The right to be awarded and hold in force certificates for Scientology and Dianetics training, internship and processing services successfully completed
* Eligibility for professional rates on processing services
* Eligibility for training scholarship awards
* Eligibility for appointment as a Field Staff Member
* Special rates on membership fees for the "I Want to Go OT" Club
* Special rates on Dianetics and Scientology materials and services —including a 20 percent discount on books, tapes and E-Meters.

These benefits are now available only to members of the International Association of Scientologists.

A free six-month membership is extended to beginning Scientologists only—those buying their first book or their first training or processing service.

Apply to the Membership Officer at your nearest Church of Scientology today. Or write directly to the *International Association of Scientologists,* c/o Saint Hill Manor, East Grinstead, Sussex, England RH19 4JY.

"I am always happy to hear from my readers."

L. Ron Hubbard

These were the words of L. Ron Hubbard, who was always very interested in hearing from his friends and readers. He made a point of staying in communication with everyone he came in contact with over his fifty-year career as a professional writer, and he had thousands of fans and friends that he corresponded with all over the world.

The publishers of L. Ron Hubbard's works wish to continue this tradition and welcome letters and comments from you, his readers, both old and new.

Additionally, the publishers will be happy to send you information on anything you would like to know about Ron, his extraordinary life and accomplishments and the vast number of books he has written.

Any message addressed to the Author's Affairs Director at Bridge Publications will be given prompt and full attention.

Bridge Publications, Inc.
4751 Fountain Avenue
Los Angeles, California 90029
U.S.A.

Church and Organization Address List

United States of America

Albuquerque
Church of Scientology
8106 Menaul NE
Albuquerque, New Mexico 87110

Ann Arbor
Church of Scientology
301 North Ingalls Street
Ann Arbor, Michigan 48104

Austin
Church of Scientology
2200 Guadalupe
Austin, Texas 78705

Boston
Church of Scientology
448 Beacon Street
Boston, Massachusetts 02115

Buffalo
Church of Scientology
47 West Huron Street
Buffalo, New York 14202

Chicago
Church of Scientology
3011 North Lincoln Avenue
Chicago, Illinois 60657

Cincinnati
Church of Scientology
215 West 4th Street, 5th Floor
Cincinnati, Ohio 45202

Columbus
Church of Scientology
167 East State Street
Columbus, Ohio 43215

Dallas
Church of Scientology
Celebrity Centre Dallas
8501 Manderville Lane
Dallas, Texas 75231

Denver
Church of Scientology
375 South Navajo Street
Denver, Colorado 80223

Detroit
Church of Scientology
321 Williams Street
Royal Oak, Michigan 48067

Honolulu
Church of Scientology
1100 Alakea Street #301
Honolulu, Hawaii 96813

Kansas City
Church of Scientology
3619 Broadway
Kansas City, Missouri 64111

Las Vegas
Church of Scientology
846 East Sahara Avenue
Las Vegas, Nevada 89104

Las Vegas *(cont.)*
Church of Scientology
Celebrity Centre Las Vegas
1100 South 10th Street
Las Vegas, Nevada 89104

Long Island
Church of Scientology
330 Fulton Avenue
Hempstead, New York 11550

Los Angeles and vicinity
Church of Scientology
4810 Sunset Boulevard
Los Angeles, California 90027

Church of Scientology
1451 Irvine Boulevard
Tustin, California 92680

Church of Scientology
263 East Colorado Boulevard
Pasadena, California 91101

Church of Scientology
10335 Magnolia Boulevard
North Hollywood, California 91601

Church of Scientology
American Saint Hill Organization
1413 North Berendo Street
Los Angeles, California 90027

Church of Scientology
American Saint Hill Foundation
1413 North Berendo Street
Los Angeles, California 90027

Church of Scientology
Advanced Organization of
   Los Angeles
1306 North Berendo Street
Los Angeles, California 90027

Church of Scientology
Celebrity Centre International
5930 Franklin Avenue
Hollywood, California 90028

Miami
Church of Scientology
120 Giralda Avenue
Coral Gables, Florida 33134

Minneapolis
Church of Scientology
3019 Minnehaha Avenue
Minneapolis, Minnesota 55406

New Haven
Church of Scientology
909 Whalley Avenue
New Haven, Connecticut 06515

New York City
Church of Scientology
227 West 46th Street
New York City, New York 10036

Church of Scientology
Celebrity Centre New York
65 East 82nd Street
New York City, New York 10028

Orlando
Church of Scientology
710-A East Colonial Drive
Orlando, Florida 32803

Philadelphia
Church of Scientology
1315 Race Street
Philadelphia, Pennsylvania 19107

Phoenix
Church of Scientology
4450 North Central Avenue, Suite 102
Phoenix, Arizona 85012

Portland
Church of Scientology
1536 Southeast 11th Avenue
Portland, Oregon 97214

Church of Scientology
Celebrity Centre Portland
709 Southwest Salmon Street
Portland, Oregon 97205

Sacramento
Church of Scientology
825 15th Street
Sacramento, California 95814

San Diego
Church of Scientology
701 "C" Street
San Diego, California 92101

San Francisco
Church of Scientology
83 McAllister Street
San Francisco, California 94102

San Jose
Church of Scientology
3604 Stevens Creek Boulevard
San Jose, California 95117

Santa Barbara
Church of Scientology
524 State Street
Santa Barbara, California 93101

Seattle
Church of Scientology
2004 Westlake Avenue
Seattle, Washington 98121

St. Louis
Church of Scientology
9510 Page Boulevard
St. Louis, Missouri 63132

Tampa
Church of Scientology
4809 North Armenia Avenue, Suite 215
Tampa, Florida 33603

Clearwater
Church of Scientology
Flag® Service Organization
210 South Fort Harrison Avenue
Clearwater, Florida 33516

Washington, DC
Founding Church of Scientology
2125 "S" Street NW
Washington, DC 20008

Canada

Edmonton
Church of Scientology
10349 82nd Avenue
Edmonton, Alberta
Canada T6E 1Z9

Kitchener
Church of Scientology
8 Water Street North
Kitchener, Ontario
Canada N2H 5A5

Montreal
Church of Scientology
4489 Papineau Street
Montréal, Québec
Canada H2H 1T7

Ottawa
Church of Scientology
150 Rideau Street, 2nd Floor
Ottawa, Ontario
Canada K1N 5X6

Quebec
Church of Scientology
226 St-Joseph est
Québec, Québec
Canada G1K 3A9

Toronto
Church of Scientology
696 Yonge Street
Toronto, Ontario
Canada M4Y 2A7

Vancouver
Church of Scientology
401 West Hastings Street
Vancouver, British Columbia
Canada V6B 1L5

Winnipeg
Church of Scientology
Suite 125—388 Donald Street
Winnipeg, Manitoba
Canada R3B 2J4

United Kingdom

Birmingham
Church of Scientology
80 Hurst Street
Birmingham
England B5 4TD

Brighton
Church of Scientology
Dukes Arcade, Top Floor
Dukes Street
Brighton, Sussex
England

East Grinstead
Saint Hill Foundation
Saint Hill Manor
East Grinstead, West Sussex
England RH19 4JY

Advanced Organization Saint Hill
Saint Hill Manor
East Grinstead, West Sussex
England RH19 4JY

Edinburgh
Hubbard Academy of Personal
  Independence
20 Southbridge
Edinburgh, Scotland EH1 1LL

London
Church of Scientology
68 Tottenham Court Road
London, W1P 0BB England

Manchester
Church of Scientology
258 Deansgate
Manchester, England M3 4BG

Plymouth
Church of Scientology
41 Ebrington Street
Plymouth, Devon
England PL4 9AA

Sunderland
Church of Scientology
51 Fawcett Street
Sunderland, Tyne and Wear
England SR1 1RS

Austria

Vienna
Church of Scientology
Mariahilfer Strasse 88A/II/2
A-1070 Vienna, Austria

Belgium

Brussels
Church of Scientology
45A, rue de l'Ecuyer
1000 Bruxelles, Belgium

Denmark

Aarhus
Church of Scientology
Guldsmedegade 17, 2
8000 Aarhus C, Denmark

Copenhagen
Church of Scientology
Store Kongensgade 55
1264 Copenhagen K, Denmark

Church of Scientology
Vesterbrogade 23 A – 25
1620 Copenhagen V, Denmark

Church of Scientology
Advanced Organization Saint Hill for
  Europe and Africa
Jernbanegade 6
1608 Copenhagen V, Denmark

France

Angers
Church of Scientology
10–12, rue Max Richard
49000 Angers, France

Clermont-Ferrand
Church of Scientology
2 Pte rue Giscard de la Tour Fondue
63000 Clermont-Ferrand, France

Lyon
Church of Scientology
3, place des Capucins
69001 Lyon, France

Paris
Church of Scientology
65, rue de Dunkerque
75009 Paris, France

Church of Scientology
Celebrity Centre Paris
69, rue Legendre
75017 Paris, France

St. Etienne
Church of Scientology
24, rue Marengo
42000 St. Etienne, France

Germany

Berlin
Church of Scientology e.V.
Sponholzstrasse 51/52
1000 Berlin 41, Germany

Düsseldorf
Church of Scientology
Friedrichstrasse 28
4000 Düsseldorf, West Germany

Frankfurt
Church of Scientology
Darmstadter Landstr. 119–125
6000 Frankfurt/Main, West Germany

Hamburg
Church of Scientology e.V.
Steindamm 63
2000 Hamburg 1, West Germany

Church of Scientology
Celebrity Centre Hamburg
Mönckebergstrasse 5
2000 Hamburg 1
West Germany

Munich
Church of Scientology e.V.
Beichstrasse 12
D-8000 München 40, West Germany

Greece

Athens
Applied Philosophy Center of Greece
(K.E.F.E.)
Ippokratous 175B
114 72 Athens, Greece

Israel

Tel Aviv
Scientology and Dianetics College
7 Salomon Street
Tel Aviv 66023, Israel

Italy

Brescia
Church of Scientology
Dei Tre Laghi
Via Fratelli Bronzetti N. 20
25125 Brescia, Italy

Milano
Church of Scientology
Via Abetone, 10
20137 Milano, Italy

Monza
Church of Scientology
Via Cavour, 5
20052 Monza, Italy

Novara
Church of Scientology
Corso Cavallotti No. 7
28100 Novara, Italy

Nuoro
Church of Scientology
Corso Garibaldi, 108
08100 Nuoro, Italy

Padua
Church of Scientology
Via Mameli 1/5
35131 Padova, Italy

Pordenone
Church of Scientology
Via Montereale, 10/C
33170 Pordenone, Italy

Rome
Church of Scientology
Via di San Vito, 11
00185 Roma, Italy

Turin
Church of Scientology
Via Guarini, 4
10121 Torino, Italy

Verona
Church of Scientology
Vicolo Chiodo No. 4/A
37121 Verona, Italy

Netherlands

Amsterdam
Church of Scientology
Nieuwe Zijds Voorburgwal 271
1012 RL Amsterdam, Netherlands

Norway

Oslo
Church of Scientology
Storgata 9
0155 Oslo 1, Norway

Portugal

Lisbon
Instituto de Dianética
Rua Actor Taborde 39–4°
1000 Lisboa, Portugal

Spain

Barcelona
Dianética
Calle Pau Claris 85, Principal 1ª
08010 Barcelona, Spain

Madrid
Asociación Civil de Dianética
Montera 20, Piso 2
28013 Madrid, Spain

Sweden

Göteborg
Church of Scientology
Norra Hamngatan 4
S-411 14 Göteborg, Sweden

Malmö
Church of Scientology
Stortorget 27
S-211 34 Malmö, Sweden

Stockholm
Church of Scientology
Kammakargatan 46
S-111 60 Stockholm, Sweden

Switzerland

Basel
Church of Scientology
Herrengrabenweg 56
4054 Basel, Switzerland

Bern
Church of Scientology
Effingerstrasse 25
CH-3008 Bern, Switzerland

Geneva
Church of Scientology
4, rue du Léman
1201 Genève, Switzerland

Lausanne
Church of Scientology
10, rue de la Madeleine
1003 Lausanne, Switzerland

Zurich
Church of Scientology
Badenerstrasse 294
CH-8004 Zürich, Switzerland

Australia

Adelaide
Church of Scientology
24 Waymouth Street
Adelaide, South Australia 5000
Australia

Brisbane
Church of Scientology
2nd Floor, 106 Edward Street
Brisbane, Queensland 4000
Australia

Canberra
Church of Scientology
Suite 16, 108 Bunda Street
Canberra Civic
A.C.T 2601, Australia

Melbourne
Church of Scientology
44 Russell Street
Melbourne, Victoria 3000
Australia

Perth
Church of Scientology
39–41 King Street
Perth, Western Australia 6000
Australia

Sydney
Church of Scientology
201 Castlereagh Street
Sydney, New South Wales 2000
Australia

Church of Scientology
Advanced Organization Saint Hill
  Australia, New Zealand and
  Oceania
19–37 Greek Street
Glebe, New South Wales 2037
Australia

Japan

Tokyo
Scientology Tokyo Org
101 Toyomi Nishi Gotanda Heights
2-13-5 Nishi Gotanda
Shinagawa-Ku
Tokyo, Japan 141

New Zealand

Auckland
Church of Scientology
2nd Floor, 44 Queen Street
Auckland 1, New Zealand

Africa

Bulawayo
Church of Scientology
74 Abercorn Street
Bulawayo, Zimbabwe

Cape Town
Church of Scientology
5 Beckham Street
Gardens
Cape Town 8001, South Africa

Durban
Church of Scientology
57 College Lane
Durban 4001, South Africa

Harare
Church of Scientology
First Floor State Lottery Building
P.O. Box 3524
Corner Speke Avenue and
 Julius Nyerere Way
Harare, Zimbabwe

Johannesburg
Church of Scientology
Security Building, 2nd Floor
95 Commissioner Street
Johannesburg 2001, South Africa

Church of Scientology
101 Huntford Building
40 Hunter Street
Cnr. Hunter & Fortesque Roads
Yeoville 2198
Johannesburg, South Africa

Port Elizabeth
Church of Scientology
2 St. Christopher
27 Westbourne Road
Port Elizabeth 6001, South Africa

Pretoria
Church of Scientology
"Die Meent Arcade," 2nd Level,
 Shop 43b
266 Pretorius Street
Pretoria 0002, South Africa

Latin America

Colombia

Bogotá
Centro Cultural de Dianética
Carrera 19 No. 39–55
Apartado Aereo 92419
Bogotá, D.E. Colombia

Mexico

Estado de México
Instituto Tecnologico de Dianética,
 A.C.
Reforma 530, Lomas
México D.F., C.P. 11000

Guadalajara
Organización Cultural Dianética de
 Guadalajara, A.C.
Av. Lopez Mateos Nte. 329
Sector Hidalgo
Guadalajara, Jalisco, México

Mexico City
Asociación Cultural Dianética, A.C.
Hermes No. 46
Colonia Crédito Constructor
03940 México 19, D.F.

Instituto de Filosofia Aplicada, A.C.
Durango #105
Colonia Roma
06700 México D.F.

Instituto de Filosofia Aplicada, A.C.
Plaza Rio de Janeiro No. 52
Colonia Roma
06700 México D.F.

Organización, Desarrollo y
 Dianética, A.C.
Providencia 1000
Colonia Del Valle
C.P. 03100 México D.F.

Centro de Dianética Polanco
Insurgentes Sur 536, 1er piso
 Esq. Nogales
Colonia Roma Sur C.P.
06700 México D.F.

Venezuela

Valencia
Asociación Cultural Dianética de
 Venezuela, A.C.
Ave. 101 No. 150–23
Urbanizacion La Alegria
Apartado Postal 833
Valencia, Venezuela

295

To obtain any books or cassettes by L. Ron Hubbard which are not available at your local organization, contact any of the following publishers:

Bridge Publications, Inc.
4751 Fountain Avenue
Los Angeles, California 90029

Continental Publications Liaison Office
696 Yonge Street
Toronto, Ontario
Canada M4Y 2A7

New Era Publications International
ApS
Store Kongensgade 55
1264 Copenhagen K, Denmark

Era Dinámica Editores, S.A. de C.V.
Alabama 105
Colonia Nápoles
C.P. 03810 México, D.F.

NEW ERA Publications, Ltd.
78 Holmethorpe Avenue
Redhill, Surrey RH1 2NL
United Kingdom

N.E. Publications Australia Pty. Ltd.
2 Verona Street
Paddington, New South Wales 2021
Australia

Continental Publications Pty. Ltd.
P.O. Box 27080
Benrose 2011
South Africa

NEW ERA Publications Italia Srl
Via L.G. Columella, 12
20128 Milano, Italy

NEW ERA Publications GmbH
Otto—Hahn—Strasse 25
6072 Dreieich 1, Germany

NEW ERA Publications France
111, Boulevard de Magenta
75010 Paris, France

New Era Publications España, S.A.
C/De la Paz, 4/1° dcha
28012 Madrid, Spain

New Era Japan
5-4-5-803 Nishigotanda
Shinagawa-Ku
Tokyo, Japan 141